Conversations in the Cognitive Neurosciences

Conversations in the Cognitive Neurosciences

edited by Michael S. Gazzaniga

A Bradford Book
The MIT Press
Cambridge, Massachusetts
London, England

This book was set in Baskerville by Graphic Composition, Inc. and was printed and bound in the United States of America.

Library of Congress Cataloging-in-Publication Data

Conversations in the cognitive neurosciences / edited by Michael S. Gazzaniga.
     p.   cm.
"A Bradford Book."
ISBN 0-262-57117-X (pbk.: alk. paper).
1. Cognitive neuroscience.   I. Gazzaniga, Michael S.
QP365.5.C66   1997
153—dc20   96–28258
                                                     CIP

Contents

Preface   *vii*

I
Basic Neuroscience Approaches to Cognition

1
Neurochemical   *3*
Floyd E.Bloom

2
Brain Imaging   *15*
Marcus E. Raichle

II
Attentional and Perceptual Processes

3
Attention   *37*
Michael I. Posner

4
Perceptual Processes   *53*
William T. Newsome

III
Neural Basis of Memory

5
Neurons and Memory   *71*
Randy Gallistel

6
Human Memory   *91*
Endel Tulving

IV
Language

7
Evolutionary Perspectives   *111*
Steven Pinker

8
Brain and Language   *131*
Alfonso Caramazza

V
Imagery and Consciousness

9
Mental Imagery   *155*
Stephen M. Kosslyn

10
Qualia   *175*
Daniel C. Dennett

Preface

Science is hard work. It is also an endeavor that is inherently cautious and measured. All too often what seems to be a clear answer to a problem in one context surfaces as a poor interpretation in another. Scientists know this and because of this fact they usually try to stay close to their data when discussing their results in scholarly publications. That is how it should be.

At the same time, the stuff that drives scientists into their laboratories instead of onto the golf links is the passion to answer questions, hopefully important questions, about the nature of nature. Getting a fix on important questions and how to think about them from an experimental point of view is what scientists talk about, sometimes endlessly. It is those conversations that thrill and motivate. And yet, most of these exchanges are lost rather than being captured for the student.

One evening several years ago we were ending one of our dinner parties that my wife and I host when a speaker comes to town. We love these evenings, as they represent a time when we can pursue a topic with our guests with all gloves off. After one such occasion a friend remarked that it was a pity not to have the conversations somehow available for others. It had been a particularly lively evening. It was then I thought of doing interviews with famous scientists for the *Journal of Cognitive Neuroscience*.

Over the past few years I have carried out a number of interviews on topics that range from molecular mechanisms to philosophical issues. Each interview has been managed on e-mail, the new glue that binds us all. Overall they take about 10 days to complete, after which the participant and I review the product and make small adjustments. Most of it, however, is not changed a whit, and out of that comes a spontaneity and zip from the interviewees that makes for good reading and gives great insight into the way they think.

The *Journal* will continue to do these interviews. We decided, however, we were at a point where they should be brought together as a unit for the public to enjoy.

Michael S. Gazzaniga
Program in Cognitive Neuroscience
Dartmouth College

I

Basic Neuroscience Approaches to Cognition

1

Neurochemical
Floyd E. Bloom

Floyd E. Bloom, M.D., is Chairman of the Department of Neuro-pharmacology at The Scripps Research Institute (our new name after July 1, 1991). He was educated at Southern Methodist University and Washington University School of Medicine, with postgraduate training at Barnes Hospital in St. Louis, and the National Institute of Mental Health (NIMH). He held faculty positions at Yale University before returning to the NIMH to head the Section on Cytochemical Neuropharmacology, the Laboratory of Neuropharmacology, and the Division of Special Mental Health Research. Before his current affiliation with Scripps, he headed the Center for Behavioral Neurobiology at the Salk Institute.

Bloom's interests are wide-ranging, but all deal with a desire to understand the brain's operations in molecular and cellular terms, both normally and in pathological circumstances, and to devise means to restore healthful operations. His current efforts include studies on the central nervous system's reactions to alcohol, the mechanisms of AIDS dementia, and the molecular basis for neutral specificity. He is a member of the National Academy of Sciences, the Institute of Medicine, the American Philosophical Society, the Royal Swedish Academy of Sciences, past President of the Society for Neurosciences and the American College of Neuro-Psychopharmacology, and Past-President of the Research Society on Alcoholism.

MG: The problem of drug addiction consumes much of our culture's energy. There are those who feel that the calm scientific analysis of the problem is not possible, mainly because hard science has little to say about the issue. As a neurobiologist, how do you view the problem and where does neurobiology fit into the current discussions?

FEB: From the perspective of a neurobiologist, all drug actions, including those of abused drugs, are based on well-characterized cellular sites and molecular mechanisms of action. The changes in cellular activity produced by these drugs lead to changes in sensory processing, motivation, attention, and arousal. Pharmacology attributes reinforcing responses, or "pleasure," to the complex set of drug-derived internal cues. All of that integrates into the perceived drug response that can motivate subsequent drug seeking behaviors. There are two more phases of the drug-brain interaction that need to be noted: (1) the adaptations that may lead to tolerance to the information-processing confusion induced by the drug effects, and (2) the subsequent long-term craving for the drug. If we are ever to find ways to help addicted humans beat their long-term problem, we must understand far more thoroughly the nature of what brain systems (transmitters, cells, and circuits) underlie drug craving. At the present we know a lot of transmitters that mediate the acute drug reinforcement of opiates and psychostimulants, but really nothing solid about the events that are taking place when a person remembers the initial reinforcing events of a previous drug-taking trial and tries to deal with the decision to use, or not to use.

MG: But, is that doable? After all, one assumes drugs are tweaking the reinforcement systems of the brain, the same reinforcement systems that are essential for any sense of pleasure, or reinforcement. If drugs were developed that blocked action on these reinforcement systems, would that not block normal mechanisms for reinforcement as well?

FEB: Our understanding of "reinforcement" mechanisms has also progressed a great deal, and it is probably no longer accurate to consider there to be one and only one such system. Insofar as these major drug types are concerned, there are some shared features of "pleasure" that may employ a common underlying general reinforcement, but the primary avenues for the initiation of the reinforcement perception arise uniquely for the drug. In my interpretation, the ways in which opiates initiate their form of pleasure are unique from those "tweaked" by psychostimulants of the drugs exemplified by cocaine, amphetamine, and congeners, and those are still separate from the ways in which caffeine or nicotine do their trick. Beyond the primary site and mechanisms of initial response, the other main place in which I believe there is a feasible approach is the remembrance of the pleasured response, which together with its environmentally dependent associations creates the craving scenario. In my concept of this scene, the present data provide opportunities to separate drug-induced reinforcement from reinforcement generally, and to deal with drug craving without canceling human memory. There is also some hope that the piece in the middle may also be manipulatable: George Koob and his colleagues presented data at the 1991 Neuroscience meeting that some dopamine blockers can interrupt cocaine reinforcement and not food reinforcement, and vice versa.

MG: That is a very strong and intriguing claim. It does suggest therapies might be developed to inhibit the reinforcing properties of particular agents. However, are we not left with the larger problem of individual needs? In other words, isn't it the case the user is still seeking ways to increase their sense of self by being reinforced by something in these artificial ways? If you find a way of blocking their highs from cocaine, won't they find their highs from alcohol? It is known that when one cures a cocaine addict, they generally move the person over into the alcoholism category.

FEB: There is no denying the clinical evidence that for many people on their way into the drug seeking pattern there is progression from cigarettes and alcohol to other more powerful uppers and downers. The primary pharmacology here is more or less drug selective, and the transitions and motivations to go on are probably unique to individuals in terms of their propensities for risk-taking, harm avoidance, or desire for internal rewards or external rewards, such as peer pressure and acceptance. Robert Cloninger at Washington University has found these "personality" qualities assessed in young boys can accurately predict their drug taking status fifteen years later.

Moving out of illegal drugs back to socially approved (and taxable) drugs may have a reverse sequence, although those are not data that I know about. However, the more fundamental answer to your question is that in my view the ultimate answer for a person who has become drug dependent is not another drug, at least in the long run, but rather the identification of the internally perceived problems that drove them to be drug seekers rather than accepting natural rewards (food, sex, money, fame, etc.).

The recent findings of a high incidence of serious mental illness in drug abusers and vice versa suggest that there may be significant mixtures of psychopathology, especially depression, in drug users. The self-termed normal user is in essence walking a very precarious tightrope in trying to "use" drugs recreationally without entering the domain of tolerance and dependence, and the false belief that they can stop whenever they want to.

The admittedly dependent person has already crossed over, and is the person toward whom the current treatment emphasis has been directed; drying them out, and then trying to find better ways to defer long-term recidivism within the environmental situation that spawned their dependency. No therapy could be considered as either ideal or even practical, if it destroyed the subject's ability to have internal reinforcement; such a state of anhedonia is in fact a major symptom in some types of schizophrenia.

MG: OK, but in a larger sense what we are trying to get at here is a science-society interaction issue. The question is whether, and if so, how neuroscience research might help evaluate the society cost effectiveness of the amounts the government is spending to reduce the supply of illegal recreational drugs. If, as the NIDA data say, only 2 percent or so of Americans "deal" or use illicit drugs regularly, is it possible to figure out which of the many more one-time trial users are likely to have a real problem with continued use, and which are likely to go on about their entertainment business without becoming addicted?

FEB: Yes, there are signs that we can predict which of a dozen individuals, when given the chance to take all the intravenous amphetamine they want, will go for it, and which, after a few buzzes, will say no thanks. The answers that impress me come from Michael LeMoal at the University of Bordeaux, who noticed that only about half of the rats who learned to give themselves amphetamine by poking their noses through specially marked holes in their test cage showed the feature of "sensitization" in which the same drug dose on subsequent days produces greater and greater locomotor activation. In trying to figure out what was different about the ones who did and did not show this effect, he noticed that when the rats were prescreened for their willingness to explore a new cage environment, and for their adrenal corticosteroid secretion patterns in this novel test cage, those who went on to show the sensitization response were more vigorous explorers and showed higher steroid secretion peaks than those who did not. The low steroid secretors–low explorers also showed less and less interest in getting their amphetamine, and so after five or six days, they just ignored the opportunity to take the drug, while the high secretors–high explorers were increasing their doses, getting more excited, and getting more drug to get even more excited. Mary Jeanne Kreek at Rockefeller has noticed similar findings in their cocaine abusers.

This could be interpreted in several ways, many of which are testable: high environmental stress might elevate one's secretion patterns, increase exploration (looking for a way out), and the double enhancement sensitizes the reward system to a hit of psychostimulant, which then mutually accelerates the whole cycle. Some may be genetically prone to being hyperreactors (or hypo); or concurrent mental illness, like depression, may emulate parts of the endocrine drive, and increase the risk of drug effects leading to dependency in individuals who might otherwise be able to decide not to use again and again.

MG: Yes, but again, are we dealing with such a complex set of issues—mental illnesses, sociopaths, homelessness, poverty, and ill-defined aspirations—that it is impossible to think of a simple biomedical remedy?

FEB: This is not unlike one of the earlier questions, but maybe we can approach it from another angle. There are three parts to the "drugs against drugs of abuse" conundrum: (1) finding drugs that will prevent the drug's initial reinforcement action to reduce the probability that casual users would find them rewarding, or that repeated abusers would continue if there was no reward, (2) in the case of heroin abusers, nicotine smokers, and alcoholics where drug-free periods immediately after periods of high-frequency use lead to immediate withdrawal symptoms, treatment with partial agonists would reduce the negative reward of the withdrawal, and unless the system could adapt to the drug-free state quickly, would substitute a no-reward drug for a reward-driven drug, and (3) drugs that could prevent long-term recidivism, long after the last drug use, often precipitated by subconscious environmental or social cues. Number 1 is constrained by the fact that while such antagonists now exist, taking them routinely, or adding them to the drinking water to reduce accidental exposure and reward carries longer term health risk (such as a parkinsonian-like disorder if taking antidopamine drugs) as well as the possibility of leading to anhedonic zombies, since the natural reward systems have long-term survival value. The other two are constrained by the issue of voluntary compliance, which is at best irregular until the individual with the problem decides for themselves to deal with it seriously, and for a long enough period of dedicated dealing that they can get straight and stay straight.

While we know a lot about the kinds of transmitters and actions that go into the drug-induced rewards for opiates, psychostimulants, nicotine, and to some degree ethanol, we know nothing at all about the other drugs yet (PCP, THC, LSD), nor about the longer term craving effect and its ability to be triggered by environmental cues. I think understanding those chemical circuits could augment the future anti-drug treatment armamentarium.

MG: Can neuroscience illuminate the real cost to the drug victim, which is not necessarily the long-term loss of neurons as with chronic excessive ethanol consumption, or the loss of life due to cancer or cardiovascular disease with smoking, but rather the retreat into the drugged state that robs them of their human intellect? Here we are talking about the subset of addicts that is not otherwise mentally disturbed.

FEB: This is not something that I can speak to from my research reading, but I am aware that the social caste system in India has, to some degree, been maintained by the use of bhang as a reward; it is a hashish-like beverage that keeps the workers satisfied with not very much monetary reward, and in a sort of endless semi-stupor; this is not a lot different than the cholinergic stupor of the zombies, or the work-harder-for-your-coca-leaves approaches in the Caribbean and South America. Sure, there are a few people whose ability to create art and fiction while on drugs is well documented, and even a few physicians with well-documented habits while still being physicians. But the odds seem to be quite against this safe-status passage as Goldstein and Kalant pointed out in their *Science* paper last year.

MG: But that is not true, according to NIDA's own statistics. Most people do walk away from drug use. Remember, for every 100 people who try drugs only two stay with it.

FEB: I think we have to distinguish between those who really tried it only once or twice and walked away, and those who try a pattern of frequent use under the belief that they can "quit any time they want to." As I read Goldstein and Kalant, there is reason to doubt the accuracy of the reports on walking away, added to which the longer one uses the less accurate one's own perceptions and drug-quitting abilities may become. As drug-use frequency increases, the brain will automatically initiate adaptive responses to overcome the drug effect. Once that happens, any withdrawal period will leave aversion-residual adaptive processes in motion unbalanced by the now absent drug. The desire to reduce that negative reinforcement with renewed drug use is sufficient motivation to keep one using. Since the systems of the brain involved here are all subcortical, the users are unlikely to be able to explain to themselves why they just broke the abstinence promises they have made.

MG: At some level you seem to be saying that because drug addicts cost us money and because of their behavior and health problems, we must try to stop them.

FEB: Yes, although the degree of that longer term burden is not easily assessed.

A loose analogy is brought to mind by the recent enactment of a law in California that all motorcyclists must now wear crash helmets. Interviews with motorcyclists revealed that most were against it, could not see the need to be constrained, and had never had an accident. One could substitute a few words here and see casual illicit drug users. Others, like motorists, felt they would feel much safer because if they did hit one of the two-wheelers their chances of going to jail for involuntary manslaughter would be reduced to an ordinary fender bender, and the cost to society for caring for the 1 percent who had problems (amounting to several thousand victims nationwide per year) would be substantially reduced. If we stop moms from abusing while pregnant, can we reduce fetal alcohol syndrome and neonatal opiate dependence? Can we reduce the number of state-supported dependent children who may be unable ever to contribute to society except by maintaining the employment rosters of prison guards and asylum custodians? Even with the legal drug alcohol, a not inconsiderable source of revenue for the federal and state governments, those non-drinkers killed by drunk drivers, generally young inexperienced drinkers, with a few old hands like Willie Shoemaker, murder more people each year than are lost to street crime or many of our smaller wars.

If we could figure out who the most susceptible were and worked to improve their chances of resisting, we might be able to revert to the libertarian attitude to drug use that prevailed 75 years ago (when Coke had real coke): if you use it alone, and do not bother anyone else, who are we to tell you not to use. The fact is, however, that we are a long way from being able to do that, and even if we were, we have very few strategies to enhance their chances of drug-free survival. Still, the amount of funding it would take to greatly increase our investment in those two objectives would probably be less than 1 percent of what we have been putting into supply interdiction. Speaking strictly for myself, I would rather the government supplied good drugs to people mandatorily enrolled in research prevention programs than to try to convince Peruvian farmers or their guerilla cosa nostra organizers that cotton sells better than cocaine.

MG: Such a scheme might be thought of as a form of legalization. Could you imagine such a plan?

FEB: Such plans have been more than imagined, they have been tried with variable reports of success and failure in the Netherlands and within the U.K. National Health Service. As long as we discuss it as drug legalization we get immediately into highly contentious and moral-based arguments where scientific fact is not going to be compelling because well-balanced controlled studies are impossible to do. But drug use could be decriminalized. The user whose productive life has been derailed could be considered more humanely, as a diagnostic pathologic entity in need of medical rehabilitation. Longer term treatment systems could be developed that might to some degree use these drugs within a conditioned behavioral adjustment protocol. Under those conditions of operation one might see that pain victims get better opiate treatment because physicians will have less fear of converting them to addiction (which is even more rare than the 2 percent who do not walk away); cocaine and amphetamine-like drugs could be used to help treat other symptoms, and marijuana could be used to help people with cancer chemotherapy nausea, glaucoma, and dysmenorrhea (in all of which it has been shown to have benefit not available through other means). If we got to that state of consideration, we might even imagine "legalization" of RU-486 to treat endocrine-dependent cancers, even though it might have additional street uses with which the citizenry takes issue. But that, I'm afraid, is a science-society issue for another chat.

2

Brain Imaging
Marcus E. Raichle

Marc Raichle is a Professor in the Departments of Radiology, Neurology, and Neurobiology at the Washington University School of Medicine. He is also a Senior Fellow in the McDonnell Center for Studies of Higher Brain Function at Washington University. He received a B. S. and M. D. from the University of Washington in Seattle and training in neurology at the New York Hospital–Cornell University Medical College where he was introduced to research on brain circulation and metabolism by Fred Plum and Jerry Posner.

He joined the faculty of Washington University in 1971 after serving two years in the United States Air Force at the School of Aerospace Medicine. His research has focused, broadly, on studies of the brain circulation and metabolism as a means of understanding human brain function in health and disease. He has been active in the development of cognitive neuroscience, serving since its inception as an advisor to the McDonnel–Pew Program in Cognitive Neuroscience. In his spare time he is an amateur oboe/English horn player, sailor, and recreational high-altitude physiologist.

MG: As one of the world's pioneers and authorities on brain imaging and, in particular, PET, how would you characterize its short history? Are the kinds of problems you think about now, the kinds you guessed you would be thinking about ten years ago?

MER: The history of modern functional brain imaging, now exemplified by a combination of PET, fMRI, and ERPs, in my mind represents a remarkably successful merging of developments in imaging technology, neuroscience, and behavior. The pieces of the puzzle had developed quite separately until about ten years ago when cognitive science joined neuroscience in using the newly developed PET techniques to measure changes in brain blood flow in relation to changes in normal human behavior. The power of this combined approach became apparent almost immediately although the learning curve remains steep.

I certainly did not envision my current scientific agenda when I began working with Fred Plum and Jerry Posner in the late 1960s on issues of brain metabolism and blood flow nor when I joined Mike Ter-Pogossian's group here at Washington University in 1971 to work with positron emitting radionuclides. I was intrigued by their unique properties for measuring regional brain metabolism and blood flow in humans. Little did I know at the time how regional and how unique. Luckily, I was in the right place at the right time as events unfolded rather quickly after my arrival in St. Louis with the introduction of X-ray CT in about 1972 and the invention of PET in our laboratory over the ensuing two years.

MG: PET was initially built to deal with medical issues, perhaps looking at cerebral stroke per se, or studying chemotherapeutic agents for brain tumor, or looking at neurotransmitters in psychiatric and degenerative disease. PET today seems mostly committed to the study of functional correlates of cognitive function. Is this true and, if so, why?

MER: Actually, at its inception PET had a very varied agenda in the minds of the people who created it. The physics and engineering people who developed the imaging devices themselves had what I would describe as a clinical nuclear medicine orientation. In my estimation they saw PET as the means by which clinical nuclear medicine could maintain a position in the clinical area along with X-ray CT, which was clearly getting all of the attention at the time. Nuclear medicine brain scans, which had been a staple of the practice of nuclear medicine, were quickly replaced by X-ray CT. Imaging had clearly captured everyone's imagination.

The people like myself who had been working with positron-emitting radio isotopes such as oxygen-15, nitrogen-13, and carbon-11 (all short-lived isotopes) for the measurement of brain blood flow, metabolism, and the like, as well as the tissue autoradiographers like Lou Sokoloff and his many disciples, all saw PET as a means of safely doing autoradiography in humans. The agenda did include the notion of functional brain mapping but, as you suggest, it included a lot else as well. There was actually a rather frustrating tension between those who thought that it ought to be tried clinically in whatever way possible and those, like myself, that felt we should be exploring what the tool could tell us about the normal brain as well as selected disease regardless of the practical clinical application.

This latter attitude might sound a bit like it's coming from someone with his head in the clouds (I know that is how it sounded to some of my nuclear medicine engineering/physics colleagues), but I remain convinced that it was the right course. The argument that I often heard was that when CT came along nobody took such a position. It was tried and it worked. Why shouldn't we do the same with PET? To me the answer was simple. CT merely did considerably better what clinicians had been doing for years with dangerous, unpleasant (for the patient), and difficult to interpret tests such as angiography and pneumoencephalography (for those who do not know or do not remember, this involved injecting air into the spinal fluid and following the resulting air bubbles through the head with X-rays—very painful for the patient as they were tipped upside-down to move the air about). Suddenly, we had the same information more accurately and without risk or discomfort to the patient. No extensive testing was needed.

With PET, on the other hand, we were suddenly handed a tool that could give us measures of blood flow, blood volume, oxygen consumption, glucose utilization, tissue pH, and receptor pharmacology, among other things. These measurements in the brain had never been a part of the clinical practice of medicine. Not only did we have to develop the methods, we had to develop an understanding of how to use the information they provided. That process is still very much ongoing and in many areas such as brain pharmacology it is a slow and tedious process. I am still optimistic that it will provide important information in a variety of areas ranging from movement disorders and psychiatric disease to certain types of brain injury. PET is, however, "competing," if you like, with many other approaches in these areas. These range from cellular and molecular techniques to various animal models.

You are absolutely right that PET and, more recently, fMRI, has established a preeminent position in the study of the functional anatomical correlates of cognitive function in humans. The wonderful relationship between blood flow and neuronal activity and the accuracy and simplicity with which PET could measure it were certainly key to its success. Once we were able to couple this to good paradigm design, thanks to the input from my good friend Michael Posner, functional imaging with PET was off and running. The final ingredient was, certainly, that the questions we could address were immensely interesting and important. This was not a technique(s) in search of a question.

MG: And now we are swamped with images and experiments concerning the pattern of activations seen with this or that cognitive task. At one level, we are at the dawn of a new era. At another level, we are also puzzling what it all means. Your group pioneered the major method used in image analysis, the subtraction method for ascertaining structure/function correlates of cognitive activity. Would you briefly review that method and describe its uses and limitations?

MER: The image subtraction methodology is best understood from an evolutionary perspective. It represents the wedding of objectives from cognitive and imaging sciences.

From an imaging perspective, the objective was to identify areas of the brain active during the performance of a particular task. Prior to the advent of the subtraction methodology, investigators using brain-imaging techniques as well as their predecessors who used simpler regional blood flow techniques (for example, people like David Ingvar, Jarl Risberg, Per Roland, and Neils Lassen) a priori decided where in the brain they would look for changes. This was the so-called "region-of-interest" or ROI approach. The brain was arbitrarily divided up according to various schemes into regions that would be analyzed for a change in blood flow or metabolism. This approach was particularly problematic when it came to the human cerebral cortex where uncertainty was the rule rather than the exception when it came to areas much beyond primary motor and sensory cortices.

The subtraction methodology changed our perspective completely. In this approach images obtained in two states (what we have come to refer to as a task state and a control state) are subtracted from one another to create a difference image. This image identifies for us those areas of the human brain that differ between the task and control states. There are no a priori assumptions about where such regions lie within the cerebral cortex or elsewhere. The subtraction images define the location and shape of the regions and also allow us to quantitate the magnitude of the change. In one sense this is an hypothesis-generating exercise; we are letting the human brain tell us how it is organized. Obviously, hypotheses generated in this matter must be tested. The solutions to this issue of hypothesis-testing have been many and consisted of simple replication approaches that we have come to favor, to various and increasingly sophisticated thresholding techniques, the first of which we also introduced some years ago. More recently, correlational techniques have been employed with fMRI.

One of the key features of the subtraction technique from an imaging perspective has been the use of a common brain space by most investigators using functional brain imaging. Provoked by our initial desire to know where we were in the brain when looking at PET images, we were drawn to the stereotaxic brain atlas of human anatomy of the French neuroradiologist Talairach and his colleagues. It had been referred to in papers by David Ingvar. After some considerable difficulty we were able to locate a copy in an obscure little book store in Paris. To this day the original atlas has not been available in the United States. A revised version published in 1988 is now widely available.

Peter Fox and Joel Perlmutter immediately set about the task of figuring out how to convert our PET images into Talairach stereotaxic space. The result was software that permitted us to take our difference images, convert them (regardless of how the subject was placed in the scanner) into a standard stereotaxic space, and average them across subjects. Results could immediately be presented in a standard format with areas of activation defined in terms of stereotaxic coordinates. While these coordinates usually refer to the central tendencies of the areas of activations, borders and volumes can be defined in this manner as well.

The use of a standard stereotaxic space is now almost universally accepted among laboratories doing functional brain imaging. In addition to the initial impact on image subtraction and averaging, the use of a standard anatomical reference has aided communication among laboratories tremendously. While many articles do refer to various Brodmann areas as well as such things as Wernicke's and Broca's areas, they also contain tables of stereotaxic coordinates that greatly aid in the resolution of ambiguities in interpreting data across experiments. This system of describing functional imaging results in terms of stereotaxic coordinates is also the basis for the creation of databases that will become increasingly powerful research tools as the world's accumulated data increase.

Thus, from an imaging perspective, the subtraction methodology involves the key steps of subtraction of images from two different brain states, registration of these results in a common, stereotaxic brain space, and averaging the results to improve the signal-to-noise properties of the images.

From an experimental point of view these developments in imaging strategy fit remarkably well with the strategies of cognitive science that were first introduced by the Dutch physiologist Franciscus Donders in 1868. As I am sure you recall, he proposed a general method for measuring internal thought processes by the time they take to perform. This very powerful approach has been expanded and exploited in ingenious ways to understand how information processing occurs in the human brain. What was so fortuitous for us was that one of the world's great practitioners and innovators of this approach, Michael Posner, had joined us at Washington University. It was a time of great excitement and innovation from both the cognitive and imaging perspectives.

While many believe that the subtraction methodology in its various versions has provided important new information about the organization of the normal human brain, it is only fair to say that it has received mixed reviews. I would just like to take this opportunity to comment on a couple of issues that have been particularly troublesome for some people.

One of the most common criticisms is that the assumption of "pure insertion" is an incorrect assumption and, therefore, the subtraction methodology is invalid. For those not familiar with this terminology, the idea of "pure insertion" assumes in general that when a task state is compared to a control state, the difference represents the addition of processing components unique to the task state without affecting processing components in the control state. The issue is, how do we know this to be true? In imaging we can ask, additionally, whether this is even an important question.

This criticism is as old as the ideas of Donders! It has been argued in the literature almost since the introduction of his technique. While successful arguments and strategies can and have been advanced for the subtraction method in cognitive science, these arguments are substantially strengthened by the introduction of functional brain imaging. If strategies change in a functional brain-imaging experiment, one can reasonably assume that brain function will also change and be manifest in the resulting images.

For example, consider two scenarios. In the first, the control state and the task state are different only by the addition of the brain-processing components unique to the task state. Everything used in the control state remains unchanged. A subtraction image under such circumstances will predictably reveal areas of increased brain activity unique to the task state without changes in areas known to be used in the control state.

Now let us consider a second scenario in which the notion of pure insertion is violated. Under these circumstances an area or areas of brain active in the control state are not active in the task state. Now the subtraction image not only reveals areas of increased activity relative to the task state but also areas of decreased activity reflecting areas used in the control state but not in the task state. Far from presenting us with a frustrating dilemma of interpretation, such data provide us with an even richer and less ambiguous understanding of human brain functional organization.

Obviously, I have oversimplified the situation somewhat to make a point. Thus, areas of the brain as seen by today's imaging techniques are not always "on" or "off:" they may be graded. This has been nicely shown in a number of experiments.

A second major criticism of the subtraction method has centered around the issue of averaging. Averaging, of course, is used to enhance the signal-to-noise properties of the images and is common to both PET and fMRI. Initially the nay-sayers suggested, despite considerable empirical imaging data to the contrary, that subtraction-image averaging would not work because of "obvious" individual differences among subjects. I am just glad we did not hear this criticism before we got started. If individual differences had been the methodological limitation portrayed by some, this entire enterprise would never have gotten off the ground floor! The vast amount of functional imaging data now available and accumulating at an almost exponential rate belies this concern.

So, does this mean that individual differences do not exist? Hardly. One has only to inspect individual human brains to appreciate that they do differ. However, general organizing principles do emerge that transcend these differences. This coupled with our increasing ability to warp images to match one another anatomically in the averaging process will further reduce the effect of these differences. I find it amusing to reflect on the fact that our initial work was aided by the relatively crude resolution of PET scanners. The blurring of data brought responses common across individuals together and allowed us to "see" them. Early on, even robust responses could be caused to "disappear" when one attempted to go to too high a resolution.

I have one final and related point to this long-winded answer to your question. This relates to the point made by some that across-subject averaging was somehow forced upon us by the limitation of PET. This assertion is simply incorrect. Within-subject averaging, which has been especially popular with fMRI, is just as feasible as across-subject averaging with both PET and fMRI. What one chooses is a matter of the question you are asking. At the outset our objective was to understand general organizing principles of the human brain that transcend individual differences. That remains a major personal objective of mine.

MG: Of the new techniques of analyzing PET data, which ones do you believe hold the most promise and will provide converging evidence? One hears a lot about the correlational technique.

MER: Two general approaches have emerged in the analysis of PET functional imaging data. One, what I would characterize as a two-stage, hypothesis-generating, hypothesis-testing approach, is conceptually quite simple. On the basis of what I referred to earlier as an hypothesis-generating experiment or, for that matter, an experiment by someone else in the literature, you select areas of the brain of interest to you. Then you conduct a second experiment on different subjects to test their statistical significance. It sounds old-fashioned and it is, but it is powerful. It is difficult to argue with the results. Its other advantage is that you are not constrained in terms of which areas are selected in the hypothesis-generating phase of the experiment. You can use any criteria you wish, although when one is jumping off into a new area of investigation the magnitude of the response is usually a primary factor, but it need not be. The advantages you gain in flexibility and statistical power are, of course, offset by the requirement for relatively large numbers of subjects to answer specific questions. Data collection itself can often drag on for many months.

The alternative approach to the analysis of PET data is really a class of techniques that I would call thresholding techniques. With these techniques you combine your hypothesis-generating and hypothesis-testing experiments into a single experiment. Leaders in this approach have been Keith Worsley and Alan Evens in Montreal, Karl Friston in London, and Andy Holmes and Ian Ford in Glasgow following some early work done in our laboratory by Peter Fox and Mark Mintun.

These approaches attempt to establish a priori a threshold above which a response can be considered statistically significant. The trick, of course, is to overcome the problem of multiple comparisons. Images contain a vast amount of data raising the real possibility of false positives. To take a traditional approach to this problem of multiple comparisons is to risk never finding anything (we have often referred to this as being "Bonferronied to death" after the well-known

Bonferroni correction for multiple comparison). Thresholding techniques offer very sophisticated statistical approaches to this problem and clearly present an attractive means of analysis of PET functional imaging data. They have become widely available through the splendid efforts of Karl Friston and the group at the Hammersmith Hospital in London, who have produced a software package (known as "SPM" for statistical parametric maps) freely available on the Internet to interested users. Because life is simpler because of SPM, it is not surprising that they are widely used.

What is the downside? My only concern with the thresholding techniques is the degree to which they put blinders on investigators in the evaluation of their data. If all one ever looks at are thresholded images one is, in my opinion, likely to get a very sanitized view of what is really going on in the brain. I personally find it very helpful to look at the subtraction image data itself (averaged, of course). It sometimes suggests hypotheses that are quite unexpected. It is also a good yardstick of the quality of one's data, especially in experienced hands!

What I would very much like to see done is a comparison of the threshold techniques and the hypothesis-generating, hypothesis-testing approach I outlined first. It would give us a much better empirically based sense of how these techniques are performing. You can blame us, in part, for this not having been done. We probably possess some of the largest functional imaging data sets in existence and these are necessary to perform such a comparison.

All of what I have said could be applied to fMRI as well. fMRI has, however, introduced another approach to data analysis that is unique to fMRI. This is known as the correlational approach. Correlational approaches to imaging data have, of course, been used in PET. Barry Horowitz at the

NIH has pioneered this approach in which one looks for correlations among areas of the brain seen across various behavioral conditions. The idea is to look for relationships that help establish the existence of functional networks. This is an interesting approach, but has not been used widely yet. The reason for mentioning it is to allow me to make a distinction between correlations among areas, as proposed by Barry, and correlations between areas and stimulus, which is what has been developed by Peter Banditenni and others for fMRI.

The correlation approach to the analysis of fMRI simply looks for a temporal correlation between a particular input (for example, a visual stimulus) and the resulting response in the cortex. Because fMRI data are collected as a very rapid temporal sequence of scans, the activity of areas can be observed to change in a highly predictable way in each individual subject. This, coupled with the unique signal-to-noise characteristics of the fMRI data, has made the correctional techniques particularly powerful in analyzing fMRI data. The only problem I see arising is in the cognitive experiment in which there is no stimulus during the scan and no externally observable behavior (i.e., "the pure thought" experiment). This is not just a hypothetical concern. We currently have a paper in press in the *Journal of Neuroscience* using such a paradigm.

MG: A pattern of activation is determined. How should one think about it? A recent study has shown that recovered aphasics show activation in the areas surrounding the classic language areas, whereas the unrecovered patients show activation of the homologous areas in the right hemisphere. Doesn't activation in this setting suggest a brain that is trying to function, but is not getting the job done?

MER: Obviously the job is not getting done! The trick, for me at least, is to understand how to interpret such findings. My own thoughts on this matter are clearly in a state of evolution.

Until recently we had focused exclusively on studies of the normal brain. This seemed reasonable and attractive for two reasons. First, we knew little about the organization of the normal human brain and we suddenly had an opportunity hardly worth passing up. Second, I was not sure how to interpret studies in which performance was degraded by disease. For example, suppose you have established in normals that a particular task reliably activates a group of areas in the brain. Now you encounter a patient who does not perform the task at all or does so imperfectly. It does not take a rocket scientist to deduce that a functional brain image under such circumstances will differ from normals. As a result of this general line of reasoning we took the tack of looking for individuals who had lesions in areas of the brain known to be active on particular tasks from studies in normals but who could, nevertheless, perform the tasks normally. A similar approach has been taken by Richard Frackowiak in London. These studies, admittedly preliminary at this time, clearly suggest some interesting rearrangements in functional cortical architecture following brain injury. We need much more data, but I believe that such an approach has much to tell us about recovery of brain function as well as normal brain function.

I still have not answered your question about the patient who could not get the job done. While I would have dismissed this as an unattractive enterprise initially, I now am not so certain that we should not be looking at what goes on when patients are attempting a task that they cannot perform at all or at least abnormally. A degradation in performance may not only reflect the lack of contribution of a particular area of the brain due, for example, to a stroke but also to "interfering" activity in other areas that are recruited under such circumstances. Pursuit of such issues will certainly contribute to our understanding of lesion-behavioral analyses and, ultimately, we might hope, lay an even firmer foundation for useful therapeutic interventions.

MG: Well, in the normal case when one sees an activation, will there be a way of determining if it reflects excitatory or inhibitory processes on the average? Right now, since both types of activation take energy, there is no way of telling. Is that correct? Obviously this becomes very important as one begins to build models from PET and fMRI.

MER: You are absolutely correct; at present we cannot tell whether an increase in blood flow represents an energy requiring excitatory or inhibitory processes. This is an instance in which it will be necessary to utilize other sources of information to interpret the findings.

It's also probably worth commenting about some other potentially confusing issues with regard to the functional imaging signals. The first that comes to mind is the negative response in a subtraction image. While most studies focus on increases in blood flow, decreases also occur and are easily observed when the task state is subtracted from the control state. Where we already have information concerning the control state (that is, we have studied it separately as a task state), we are in a position to know whether the apparent reduction is due to a reduction in an area selectively activated in the control state and not in the task state. Alternatively, we occasionally see a reduction in an area not selectively activated in the control state. Interpretation of this observation is likely to be quite different. It is certainly well known from single unit recordings that reductions in cortical neuronal activity can occur from a baseline firing rate. It is not surprising that PET and fMRI might detect such changes.

Another area where our understanding of the physiology is incomplete is in the interpretation of the so-called BOLD (blood oxygen level dependent) signal in fMRI. As you probably know, the most commonly used fMRI signal is an increase in tissue oxygenation due to an increase in local blood flow in excess of the local oxygen demands of the tissue. Hence the name blood oxygen level dependent or BOLD signal. This is due to an apparent uncoupling of oxidative metabolism during functional activation within the brain. When we first observed this with PET a number of years ago it came as a complete surprise to us and was greeted with great scepticism by some. While fMRI studies have amply confirmed the phenomenon, it is important to point out that we do not understand yet why the brain does this and whether there might be any exceptions. For example, are reductions in neuronal activity from a resting baseline accompanied by a reverse BOLD signal? Does every area of the cerebral cortex behave in this manner? Is this true for both excitatory and inhibitory energy-requiring processes? While I am certainly not suggesting that we suspend work until we have answers for such questions, I do think it prudent that we keep the limits of our knowledge in mind when it comes to the interpretation of our data and also encourage others to pursue these very interesting neurobiological questions.

Finally, after all of these years we still do not know exactly how blood flow in the brain is coupled to neuronal activity as it most surely seems to be. While people interested in the vascular physiology and pharmacology of the brain have been pursuing this for many years, it is my opinion that this research has lacked, until quite recently, a true neurobiological perspective. Blood vessels are not just handy markers for use in lining up histological sections of the brain, they are important players that intimately interact with the cellular elements of the brain in a beautiful but poorly understood manner. The success of functional brain imaging will certainly depend, in part, on a complete understanding of these relationships.

MG: One of the potentially beautiful aspects of brain-imaging technologies is that, as you have said, areas are activated that were not part of the original hypothesis. New networks and populations of cells are observed to be part of a particular task. As you know, an exciting area and realization in neuroscience is that population coding must be the way to study how the brain gets its job done. Now, moving from recording from single neurons to say twenty neurons or even 100 neurons is a big leap forward. On the other hand, these are paltry numbers when compared to the number of neurons that must be activated in any PET or fMRI image where a pattern of activation across the whole cortex may involve hundreds of millions of neurons. We tend to say both approaches are sensitive to the population approach and yet they are very different. Do you have any thoughts on this?

MER: We obviously have before us different levels of analysis. They all contribute, each in their own way, to an understanding of how the brain works. While each of us chooses to work at a particular level, largely because it is impossible to do otherwise, it is vitally important that we keep our work in perspective. I am occasionally provoked by claims that this or that neuron or group of neurons is doing some rather high-level cognitive task based on unit recordings in animals.

A moment's reflection usually calls to mind a similar task, performed in humans, that elicits activity in areas widely distributed across the cortex. Interpretations of the behavior of local populations need to be constrained by such information.

Conversely, those of us working at the broad-brush level of functional imaging in humans need to be ever mindful of the work of those who do examine small populations of neurons. The information they have concerning activity at this level will be crucial in interpreting imaging data. An example comes immediately to mind. Tracking activity in the human hippocampus during functional imaging studies of memory in humans has been a bit of an embarrassment. It's been seen, but not consistently, even by the same research groups, including us! Now one could suggest a number of technical reasons for this, but my suspicion is that we have not yet come to grips with the relationship between hippocampal physiology and behavior. An even cursory examination of the work of people like Buzsaki, McHaughton, or Rolls on the complex temporal association between firing of cells in the hippocampus, or the cessation thereof, and behavior is instructive. I am not aware of studies that take into consideration such details in the design of functional imaging studies in humans. I believe attention to such details will pay big dividends.

The bottom line is that we must maintain a dialogue between levels of analysis.

MG: Finally, we are an interdisciplinary journal. What should the cognitive neuroscientists look for when they read either a PET or fMRI study? Do you have something like a checklist of things that had to be done before you take a study seriously?

MER: Because methods of analysis and techniques, especially fMRI, are still very much in a state of development, it is difficult to prescribe a set of criteria that would be generally useful in evaluating the imaging aspects of each study. What I think we have to be concerned about is the indiscriminate use of software packages to analyze data by well-meaning individuals who really do not understand what they are doing. This is difficult to discern in a paper, but often comes out in presentations. I am not entirely unsympathetic to the dilemma of young investigators struggling with the many complex technical issues these experiments often raise. We will, however, benefit greatly in the long run if the next generation of cognitive neuroscientists do understand the tools they are using.

While the technical imaging issues will remain a problem for many and will certainly lead, at times, to confusing results, it is my firm conviction that the behavioral issues in functional imaging experiments are the real Achilles heel. I am repeatedly impressed that remarkably subtle differences in behavioral design end up making large differences in the imaging results (these are surprisingly sensitive tools). Piloting of behavioral paradigms prior to actually performing imaging experiments and accurately documenting performance variables during the imaging experiment contribute greatly to these experiments. Careful reading of a paper usually reveals whether these aspects of the study receive proper attention.

II

Attentional and Perceptual Processes

3

Attention
Michael I. Posner

Michael Posner has been a Professor of Psychology at the University of Oregon since 1965. His work has generally been in the area of selective attention. During the 1960s and 1970s, Posner's work relied primarily on chronometric methods and is best described in his Paul Fitts lectures published as Chronometric Explorations of Mind. *From 1979 to 1985 Posner directed a laboratory at Good Samaritan Hospital and worked on the role of the parietal lobe and other structures involved in visual orienting. From 1985 to 1988 Posner directed a neuropsychology laboratory in St. Louis where he worked with Marc Raichle and Steve Petersen in developing PET methods appropriate to cognitive studies (see* Images of Mind *with M. Raichle). Since 1988, Posner has been working on combined spatial and temporal studies exploring the plasticity of human attention and skill acquisition. Posner's work has been recognized by membership in the U.S. National Academy of Sciences, APA's Distinguished Scientific Contribution Award and William James book award (with M. Raichle), and by the Vollum award for outstanding contribution to science and technology in the Pacific Northwest.*

MG: Sometimes it is proposed that William James really said it all, and that we are merely producing the converging evidence to support his wise words. In particular, he said:

Everyone knows what attention is. It is the taking possession of the mind, in clear and vivid form, of one out of what seem several simultaneously possible objects or trains of thought. Focalization, concentration of consciousness are of its essence. It implies withdrawal from some things in order to deal effectively with others, and is a condition which has a real opposite in the confused, dazed, scatter-brain state.

What have we learned since he made this remarkable statement?

MIP: William James had a great idea that sounds just the right themes, and I often begin my talks with this quote, but I still talk for 50 minutes! "Taking possession of the mind" unpacks to a study of higher level attention related most closely to focal experience and also to the issue of cognitive or voluntary control. What we now know is that focal attention does not necessarily block other stimuli from contacting their habitual internal representations (even their meanings) and being stored as implicit memories. But it often prevents these unselected items from access to awareness and novel responses or later explicit recall. Why? Because the act of focal attention involves a brain network and like all networks, this one becomes organized around its present activity and cannot be easily accessed by other signals. There are similar new findings around each of James' assertions.

MG: Well, there is no question that the study of attention is central to the field of cognitive neuroscience. Ever since James' observations, it has migrated from a few observations to a field almost unto itself. Several important ideas have emerged. How would you cast the evolution of the topic by decade, from the 1970s to the present?

MIP: In the last three decades an understanding of the physical basis of attention has been developed.

In the 1970s it became possible to record from cells in alert monkeys while they scanned their environment and responded to targets. Wurtz, Mountcastle, and others reported cells in a number of brain areas whose firing rates were enhanced when monkeys attended. This work could then be related to studies of orienting and other aspects of attention that had developed in the 1960s (e.g., Broadbent) as part of the effort to understand the way the brain processed information.

During the 1980s and since, the study of patients with selective lesions and scalp electrical recording established links between the brain areas showing selective enhancement and specific aspects of information processing. In the last decade neuroimaging methods confirmed and extended the types of attention that could he studied physiologically, and some of these findings began to influence computational models of attention such as those of LaBerge.

MG: Is there anything that attention does not do? And while it can impact early (sensory) or late (decision) processes, where do you think the study of attention has a greater impact?

MIP: There is a great deal attention cannot do. To give one simple example, while orienting to a location, attention can give priority to that location, so that targets that occur there are perceived more rapidly and with lower thresholds. Attention does not, however, substitute for the acuity provided by the fovea. While the fovea is critical for acuity, the costs in reaction time for an unexpected foveal stimulus are just as great as for an unexpected peripheral event. Visual attention influences priority but acuity only slightly if at all.

While visual attention is important, partly because we are closer to understanding its mechanisms, it probably plays a much smaller role in many of our lives than attention to semantic information stored in memory. We may be even more symbolic animals than we are visual animals.

MG: There have been many advances indeed. The field of attention, of course, has many subareas. People speak of spatial attention, automatic attention, attentional resources, and so on. Could you give us a brief summary of the major types of attention that are being studied in the setting of cognitive neuroscience?

MIP: The dominant function studied in the last few years has been orienting of attention toward sensory stimuli within the visual system. Orienting can be forced by stimuli (often by transient onsets) or shifted as a result of voluntary control, and it has been a vehicle for separating automatic from voluntary mechanisms. PET studies have converged with cellular and lesion results to show the importance of the parietal area together with thalamic and mid-brain areas. There are many issues being debated about how these areas work together and influence object recognition. However, there is also a great deal of agreement about visual orienting, and similar detailed analyses are starting to develop in other sensory systems.

The idea of resources refers more to higher level attentional systems related to the subjective impression of mental effort. Neuroimaging methods have shown frontal areas associated with paying attention in the sense of exerting hard mental effort. Whenever tasks appear to involve strong mental effort they have shown activation of areas of the anterior cingulate, for example, during detection of targets and the resolution of conflict such as in the Stroop task.

The topic of acquiring and maintaining alertness in the face of long, boring tasks has been an area of continued interest. Recent studies have suggested both some of the anatomy involved and the importance of modulation by norepinepherine in the alerting that follows warning signals.

MG: Let us start with orienting toward visual stimuli. While it is clear cueing to a location decreases reaction time to responding, how good is the evidence that sensitivity to perceptual details is enhanced? What I am after here is distinguishing between how attention may be useful for simple detection of events versus improving our performance at those events.

MIP: There has been a great deal of controversy over what is improved by orienting attention to a visual stimulus. It is generally agreed that the attended stimulus is given priority, so that reaction time to it is reduced. There is also clear evidence of enhancement of electrical activity over extrastriate visual areas by 80–100 msec after input. One recent study has shown that location of the ERP generator has a rough correspondence to areas to increased blood flow found in the same task.

However, it is also clear that attention to a peripheral stimulus does not compensate for the lack of acuity that would be present for a foveal stimulus. Stimuli in the fovea always have an advantage in detail, even if the priority for processing input has been given elsewhere. In an empty visual field the benefits of an attention precue are subtle, even if they can be measured at least sometimes in terms of improved RT over unattended locations. However, once the field is complex, attention is necessary to locate targets that would be completely unseen otherwise. The use of almost empty fields has been important in demonstrating attentional deficits in patients. The fact that parietal patients will not see a contralesional event following an ipsilesional invalid cue shows that the mechanisms of orienting can be a crucial step for detecting a target, even if in normal subjects we can usually measure only an increased latency.

MG: Are these effects modality-specific or hemisphere-specific? If the parietal patient's ipsilesional hand was touched (cued), would there be the same deficit?

MIP: Orienting appears to be both modality- and hemisphere-specific, but in a somewhat complex way. We know from PET studies in normals that the right parietal lobe is involved in attention shifts on either side, but the left parietal lobe appears to be involved in attention shifts only on the right side. In patients, right parietal damage appears to influence the ability to orient leftward in both visual fields. When the two hemispheres are connected as in normal persons, a single focus of orienting appears to be maintained, although when the brain is split as in the patients you have studied, there appear to be two foci of orienting, one for each hemisphere.

Visual, tactile, and auditory neglect appear to involve separate areas of the parietal lobe, but of course they are in communication, as is clear when visual information influences the location from which we hear speech (ventriloquism effect).

MG: Are there sensible reasons why the right hemisphere appears to monitor both visual fields while the left appears to monitor only the right visual field? This appears to be true from a number of studies, as you say, and also true for split-brain patients. Does that mean the monitoring involves subcortical systems, since the disconnected right hemisphere keeps track of the ipsilateral visual field?

MIP: This is a difficult question to answer. We know that arousal networks tend to be right-lateralized in humans. Our infant studies show the importance of visual orienting mechanisms in the first year of life, and this early development may give the right hemisphere, often supposed to develop earlier, an advantage over the left.

MG: So, then what is your proposed neural mechanism for visual spatial attention? While you have elegantly shown in the past that spatial attention mechanisms can be differentiated from oculomotor mechanisms (that in short it is an independent system), do you think the neural sites for managing these activities are different?

MIP: The neural systems partly overlap, but there are also important differences. Consider the role of the colliculus for example. LaBerge has proposed that it is involved when attention shifts occur between distant targets but is not involved when they involve close targets. This sounds as though the colliculus is involved when one might normally make an eye movement, but happens to move attention covertly instead. However, eye movements are always to peripheral stimuli, but attention shifts can be shifted as well to the fovea from peripheral locations, so that the mechanisms must be different in detail.

MG: People often associate your attention work with the study of spatial visual orienting. Spatial attention is frequently distinguished from object-based attention. How does your work speak to other forms of attentional orienting?

MIP: Again, this is a story of progress. I originally emphasized attention to spatial location because I was working in a nearly empty field and tried to avoid the complexity of competing objects. I realized that objects were important: after all, I also share the phenomenology that objects are what we pay attention to.

Although objects dominate perception, it still seems to me exciting to observe the assembly of features into objects by control of attention under special conditions such as those of visual search. I was delighted when Triesman's feature integration theory supported the idea that objects came later as the result of attention-integrating features. Based on these developments attention to locations and attention to objects were often taken as rivals.

Recently, however, Egly and his colleagues have provided evidence that the right hemisphere which dominates for spatial location cares more about locations than objects while it is the reverse for the left hemisphere. I was quite amazed to see that the brain actually considered in its organization what had seemed like a somewhat arbitrary distinction.

MG: Attention is itself dynamic: it can move around. Pat Cavanagh has several visual demonstrations relating to this point, but one of the most compelling is a field of perhaps a dozen swirling points. He colors some of these red and asks you to keep track of them after they are colored like the rest (the old shell game but with up to four peas and a dozen shells). With up to four present, you can do pretty well at tracking them. Thus attention follows the stimulus, even when it is moving. As a consequence of this kind of thing, he models attention as being part of the representation itself; something that "attaches" itself to the representation and facilitates the segmentation of the attended object. He names this process "sprite"—a little demon that jumps into a map, on top of the stimulus. The point is that he views attention as very low level, something happening early in the visual system. Comment?

MIP: There have been demonstrations of tracking a number of moving dots under circumstances where you can deal with the set of moving items as an object. Pylyshyn and Cavanaugh are prominent among the investigators that have studied this phenomenon. However, I doubt if Cavanaugh wants to endorse a demon as a good neural account of how the mechanism works. Having discussed a spotlight a few years ago, I know only too well how what starts as a crude metaphor can be taken as a serious viewpoint to be tested. Nonetheless I agree that the evidence suggests that attention can have an influence quite early in the visual system, and that we are still learning what visual operations attention influences.

MG: What are the significant questions that attention work has to answer?

MIP: If you think there are specific brain networks that subserve the operations of attention, exciting tasks for you to study are (1) describing the anatomy of these networks, (2) studying their real time activation, (3) examining their development, and (4) understanding what goes wrong with them in brain injury and psychopathology.

   I have addressed all of these questions. Many of the results are summarized in my book with Marc Raichle, *Images of Mind,* and subsequent publications. It has been fun, but of course, much remains undone on each of them.

MG: That marvelous book brings up the issue of how brain imaging helps us understand cognitive functions and, in particular, attention. With the plethora of new, noninvasive imaging techniques come opportunities to discover the dynamics of brain function and attentional processing. However, different techniques often measure different brain functions (fMRIs vs. ERPs for instance): isn't there a danger that different brain areas will be implicated depending on the imaging approach that is used? Wouldn't this create confusion in the field?

MIP: There are several answers to this issue. There is no reason that different measures should provide exactly the same anatomy. The vascular changes that produce the signals for fMRI and PET are themselves somewhat different, and both differ from the neuronal firings that produce electrical activity Thus we cannot expect more than general correspondence between signals. When this general correspondence fails we will need to understand why this is so. Simple explanations like differences in sensitivity could be involved, but we will have to be alert to possibly important differences not yet understood. Astronomy has gained, not lost, from the fact that optical and radio waves are not identical, and give different pictures of the universe.

As I read the PET, fMRI, and ERP literature to date it looks like the early studies provide somewhat the same picture. Perhaps that is because of the problems chosen for study. Keep in mind that there are disputes and failures to replicate, even within a method, so we will expect some continuing need to confirm and replicate studies.

MG: Isn't there a tendency for a confirmatory bias with the imaging techniques—where results that are disparate with previous findings using other techniques such as the lesion approach are rejected, and those that are consistent with previous findings are accepted? For example, the old PET finding that the cerebellum tends to light up with semantic processing—an unusual result that most considered bound to be wrong—and one that in more recent years has gone away by simply slowing down the presentation rate of the stimuli?

MIP: I do not agree with your premise. I actually think the connection between PET and lesion work has been instructive about how converging methods should proceed.

In our original PET studies we found an area of the left ventral occipital lobe that we identified with the visual word form. Immediately there was a problem because lesions of the visual word form should have caused pure alexia, but the classic theory of pure alexia was that there was both a left hemisphere lesion and a cut of the corpus callosum, producing a disconnection of the visual system from the angular gyrus. I worried a great deal about this discrepancy, but more recent lesion data seem to indicate that the left posterior lesion is sufficient.

On the other hand, PET data from the London group seemed to suggest that the word form was more anterior and lateral in the temporal lobe than we found. While this discrepancy has not been entirely clarified, it appears to be due to differences in the control task used. In any case, both cellular recording and PET data are suggesting a network of left-lateralized areas that involve letter and word processing related to the synthesis of visual letters into an orthographic code. These results fit with many cognitive theories of the same functions.

Another early discrepancy between PET and lesion data was the failure of the PET studies to show Wernicke's area during tasks related to word meanings. This was disturbing because lesion data had clearly related this area to some aspects of semantic processing. Later PET data with a slower exposure duration reconciled this discrepancy by showing that at a somewhat slower rate Wernicke's area is active. Moreover, recent ERP data have shown that the Wernicke area activation—found when comparing the generation of a new association with reading aloud—does not start until about 600 msec, while lateral frontal areas also related to generated word meanings are active by about 240 msec. This finding provides some interesting constraints on how frontal and posterior areas might share semantic functions. So once again discrepancies have provided a basis for progress.

I believe both exposure durations activated the cerebellum, which may well be crucial for generating uses of words, since lesions of the lateral cerebellum do disrupt this task just as the PET data suggest. In short, we must continue to look for convergence between imaging, lesion, and developmental data as a way of advancing our knowledge.

MG: What has attention work told us about the brain that we did not know before? Surely, it is clear that the brain has told us much about attention.

MIP: This seems to me to be the most exciting of all the issues you raise in this interview. Studies of attention suggest that our subjective experience and cognitive control are associated with specific brain networks. The special quality of these networks and how they developed in phylogeny and ontogeny become central issues of brain research of particular importance to psychology.

When subjects practice a list of associations for fifteen minutes, Marc Raichle has found that they shift pathways from those that involve focal attention networks to pathways that do not. What an incredible change. If this is a general principle, brain research needs to consider what it is about the wiring of the networks that allows for the control processes carried out by attention.

To accomplish this goal we will have to specify in detail the role of attention within some skilled act by cognitive research and then observe the anatomy and circuitry involved to determine how the structure and connections subserve the required functions. We will then have a start in understanding how the brain coordinates its own actions, a worthy goal for brain research don't you think?

MG: What about the future? Where will the big advances come in understanding attention?

MIP: In the future it will be particularly important to begin to dissociate the idea of executive function into its component operations. Some developments along these lines have already taken place.

For example, an important aspect of coherent behavior is to have a set of goals (goal tree) that can control current behavior. Recently Duncan has argued for goal neglect, in which frontal patients are less able to order and implement a set of instructed goals. It is likely that the orbital frontal area may be of central importance to this executive function. A basis for dissociating conscious experience from feelings of control arises in REM sleep. Dreaming is clearly conscious experience, but except in the rare case of so-called lucid dreaming this form of conscious behavior is not accompanied by feelings of control. While we do not know the specific brain areas involved, we have learned from the work of Hobson and others on REM sleep that it involves the reduction or loss of catecholamines such as NE and 5HT.

A number of recent theories have sought to determine the cognitive deficit from a loss of basal ganglia function. One way to characterize this deficit is to suppose that the basal ganglia are important for switching the organism between sets. Steve Keele, among others, has argued that Parkinson patients can show difficulty in turning on motor behavior or a similar reduction in ability to shift task sets depending on basal ganglia loops most involved. The basal ganglia are also the source of dopamine input to the anterior cingulate, and thus the two frontal structures have a very close relationship.

Lateral frontal areas appear to be involved in holding information that is not currently present in the front of the mind. Thus monkey studies by the Goldman-Rakic's group, PET data by Smith and Jonides, and fMRI data from Jon Cohen show the lateral frontal cortex as containing portions of working memory. The close connection between executive attention and temporary representations has played a prominent role in theories of working memory, and the close anatomical connections between the anterior cingulate and lateral areas of the frontal cortex may be the basis of this connection. All of these findings and more suggest we may be able to reduce the embarrassment caused by the idea of executive control (of postulating a homunculus) by the typical analytic strategy of science.

MG: Finally, what are you doing to study attention these days?

MIP: The studies of PET and fMRI have pointed out a specific anatomy related to aspects of selective attention. By use of a large number of scalp electrodes, it is possible to trace activation of that anatomy in real time. For example, we have seen anterior cingulate activation at about 170 msec related to higher level attention in determining the meaning of a visual word. We have studies currently underway to observe the function of the form of attention indexed by cingulate activation, how activation changes with practice, its relationship to other codes activated during reading, and when in development it starts to reflect voluntary control of behavior. To actually observe these areas studied by PET come on and off line in real time has been exciting.

MG: What do you expect a cognitive neuroscience lab, or conference, or journal will look like in ten years?

MIP: Here's my version of the table of contents of an issue of the *Journal of Cognitive Neuroscience* in 2006:

How communication between brain areas involved in first and second language comprehension changes with mastery of the new language.

At what age are genes coding for extraversion expressed?

Laser images of neuronal activity in parietal cortex during mental rotation.

Function of monkey cortex homologous to the human visual word-form system.

A pharmacological study designed to reduce loss of brain plasticity with age.

Size of brain areas devoted to the semantic categories "animal" as a function of expertise: a functional MRI study.

Change in blood flow and dopamine uptake in auditory areas following pharmacological treatment for auditory hallucinations in first-break schizophrenics.

MG: Thank you.

4

Perceptual Processes
William T. Newsome

Bill Newsome is a professor in the Department of Neurobiology at the Stanford University School of Medicine. He received his B. S. in physics from Stetson University in 1974 and his Ph.D. in biology from Caltech in 1980. Following postdoctoral work at NIH, he served on the faculty at SUNY Stony Brook before joining the Stanford faculty in 1988. His research has focused on the neural mechanisms underlying visual perception and visually guided behavior. Newsome was a co-recipient of the Rank Prize in opto-electronics in 1992, and received the Minerva Foundation's Golden Brain Award in the same year. This fall he received the Spencer Award, granted yearly by the College of Physicians and Surgeons at Columbia University for highly original contributions to research in neurobiology. In addition, he won the Kaiser Award for excellence in preclinical teaching granted annually by the Stanford School of Medicine.

MG: You were trained by a number of scientists whose expertise ranged from anatomy and cellular physiology up to psychophysics. Was there a plan here? Did you feel this broad training was a necessary process in order for you to study the kinds of questions you now examine?

WTN: I wish I could say that my current research program resulted from precocious insight, but that would be disingenuous. You are correct that my entrée to the business was through bottom-up anatomical and physiological experiments. I received excellent training in these approaches in the laboratories of John Allman and David Van Essen, and this background in the blunt realities of brain organization has served me well in ensuing years. Fortunately, though, I was influenced at a fairly early stage by several mentors who helped me realize that the bare facts of neurophysiology and anatomy come to life most incisively in the context of behavioral and psychophysical functions that the system performs. John Allman nudged me toward this line of thinking in graduate school, but I became fully committed to it only during postdoctoral work with Bob Wurtz and collaborative experiments with Tony Movshon. I now appreciate that psychophysics and behavior *define* the playing field for the physiologist. The inner workings of a complex system are most sensibly probed if we have in hand (1) a reasonably clear idea of the overall function of the system, and (2) reasonably quantitative measurements of the system's capabilities. A cardinal feature of my current work, then, is that psychophysical and physiological events are monitored and manipulated simultaneously—in the same animal, on the same sets of trials, under precisely identical conditions. Applied together, the two approaches yield keener insights than either approach alone.

MG: That is, of course, the tremendous power of the animal (primate) model. And you say that with such conviction that I cannot resist examining the other side of the coin. At what point do animal models break down? One wouldn't want to study the brain mechanisms of ennui in rats. Are there limits in visual science as to what the monkey can teach the student of human perception?

WTN: I would think there must be limits, but I doubt that we have even begun to approach them. Behavioral, anatomical, and physiological similarities suggest that we share a great deal of visually based cognition with nonhuman primates, including object recognition, visually directed navigation, spatial attention, visual memory, and simple forms of decision making. Investigation of these phenomena in alert, behaving animals has been seriously engaged relatively recently. One possible limit that does concern me is in the area of abstract representation, which humans seem to accomplish mostly through linguistic mechanisms. In our laboratory, for example, we are beginning to investigate neural mechanisms underlying a simple decision process in our motion discrimination paradigm. It is unclear, however, whether the result of a monkey's decision is registered and held only in premotor circuitry that prepares the animal's operant response, or whether the decision is implemented in a more abstract, "supramodel" circuit that then informs appropriate premotor centers. In humans, I think, the outcome of decisions can be readily held in the abstract form of a linguistic representation. In monkeys, however, the outcome of any decision may be linked much more tightly to specific actions, and thus to premotor circuitry.

MG: Yes, that relates to the old truth that when a nonmusician hears a tone to be remembered, it is assumed to be stored with perceptual parameters at work. When a musician hears the same tone (say, B-flat) she or he simply notes the referent. And surely wholly different brain mechanisms are at work with these two groups.

WTN: I would think so.

MG: But before we drop the interspecies tension, it should be noted there are growing lists of differences. For example, a rhesus monkey with the callosum sectioned, but the anterior commisure intact, transfers virtually all visual information. Yet humans with the same surgical manipulation transfer virtually no visual information. Humans with lesions of primary visual cortex most likely cannot see. Yet monkeys with the same lesion are able to see. The volume of area striata in the human is three times what it is in monkeys. And alas, can't the lowly bird with its hugely different visual system do most of what a human or primate can do with visual stimuli?

WTN: Certainly there must be differences. Some, like the interhemispheric transfer example you cite, probably reflect anatomical convenience more than basic functional differences. I suspect that interhemispheric coordination of visual information is probably similar in humans and nonhuman primates despite differences in the precise routes taken by interhemispheric axons. Other species differences, like those between birds and primates, probably entail more profound variation in information-processing strategies. I suspect we would learn a great deal about how biological vision works by understanding both the shared and the unique processing mechanisms of visual systems as strikingly different as those of primates and birds. I work on primates because the animals are so amenable to studies in which psychophysics and physiology are combined in the same experiments; we can actually prowl around inside the system while it is functioning in a reasonably normal fashion. Perhaps a clever student reading this interview will eventually show us that the same thing can be done in birds.

MG: OK, a final question dealing with the philosophy of your approach. What are the limitations of single neuron analysis? One might think that assessing the behavior of one neuron at a time would severely limit the kind of analysis you can do.

WTN: The most obvious limitation of the single unit approach is the difficulty in analyzing neural representations involving simultaneous activity at multiple locations in the brain. This limitation can, of course, be rather severe since even simple sensory stimuli or motor acts evoke complex patterns of neural activity in the brain. A second limitation, that receives somewhat less attention, is that the single unit approach provides little information about the relative timing of neural events at different locations in the brain. The timing of neural activity in different brain structures can provide critical temporal information bearing on the possibility of cause-and-effect relationships between those structures. A final limitation is that single unit recording in the central nervous system virtually precludes precise analysis of input-output transfer functions. For any given neuron, we have only the most general notion of what its inputs might be, such notions being based largely on population studies of anatomical connections and physiological properties. The strongest statements concerning transfer functions are usually of the form: "This type of response selectivity has not been observed at prior levels of the pathway, and is probably synthesized from simpler inputs for [some specific computational or behavioral purpose]."

Having criticized the single unit approach, let me hasten to add that we have not yet begun to exhaust its usefulness. Single unit analyses are still employed profitably in conjunction with anatomical techniques to identify basic processing modules in different brain structures—what Hubel and Wiesel termed "functional architecture." I suspect that this enterprise will continue to be productive, especially if molecular techniques can provide more precise anatomical markers for neural circuits. Even more exciting to me, obviously, is the recent trend toward applying the single unit approach in behaving animals trained to perform simple cognitive tasks. More laboratories are now employing clever behavioral paradigms (frequently adapted from the experimental traditions of psychophysics and behavioral psychology) to investigate neural substrates of perception, attention, learning, memory, and motor planning, to name but a few. A wealth of new insight is emerging from these efforts, and I believe we have only scratched the surface of what can be learned.

MG: OK, tell us briefly about the specific approach you take and how you use it to instruct us on how the brain enables a visual percept.

WTN: For several years we have worked in an extrastriate visual pathway that emphasizes the analysis of motion information. Our central goal has been to determine whether and how neural responses to moving visual stimuli underlie perceptual responses to the same stimuli. We chose the motion pathway not because it is intrinsically more interesting than other systems in the brain, but because we had evidence from prior single unit studies concerning the likely function of this pathway. Semir Zeki and Ron Dubner first discovered that most neurons in a region of the superior temporal sulcus are directionally selective, prompting them to suggest that this area was specialized for processing motion information. This system therefore offered a good opportunity to examine closely the relationship between neural activity and a specific perceptual capability—motion vision. Our basic approach has been to train rhesus monkeys to discriminate the direction of motion in a family of random dot displays in which the difficulty of the task can be varied continuously by modulating the strength of the motion signal in the display. We have used all the tools at our disposal—pharmacological inactivation, single unit recording, micro-stimulation, and behavioral manipulation—to explore the relationship between neural and perceptual events.

MG: For the general reader, how would you characterize your basic set of findings?

WTN: There are three salient findings of interest to the general reader. First, several laboratories have now shown that inactivation or ablation of MT can selectively impair motion vision, including performance on the direction discrimination task used in our work. While these inactivation experiments confirm a prominent role for MT in motion vision, they yield little insight into the character of the signals carried by MT neurons and how those signals are processed to yield psychophysical performance. To gain insight into these issues, we next recorded from single MT neurons while monkeys performed the direction discrimination task. One of the most surprising results of this study was that single MT neurons, on average, are as sensitive to directional signals in the stochastic visual display as is the monkey psychophysically. In other words, the responses of an average MT neuron convey enough information about the direction of stimulus motion to account for the monkey's psychophysical performance. This observation flies in the face of conventional thinking about the effects of signal averaging within pools of sensory neurons: averaging should eliminate much of the noise carried by single neurons, producing psychophysical performance superior to the sensitivity of any single neuron in the pool. We are currently engaged in a modeling study to identify conditions under which various pooling models can be reconciled with our experimental measurements of neuronal and psychophysical sensitivity. This effort is producing new insights into signal pooling within the cortex and the factors that limit fidelity of the pooled signal.

The third observation of general interest is that electrical microstimulation of directionally selective MT neurons can influence judgments of motion direction in a predictable manner. When a monkey discriminates between two opposed directions of motion in one of our stochastic stimuli, we can actually tilt his judgment in favor of one or the other alternative by electrically activating a column of MT neurons that responds optimally to one of the two directions. To obtain optimal effects, the train of stimulating pulses must occur during the brief display interval in which the monkey actually inspects the stimulus and arrives at his decision. This result is particularly important because it establishes a causal link between the activity of neural circuits identified at the single unit level and a specific visual capacity—direction discrimination. In other words, single unit properties measured with a microelectrode can be used to predict the behavioral consequences of perturbing activity within intricately organized circuits of the cerebral cortex. One can think of this result as being analogous to the molecular biological experiment of inserting a novel gene into a bacterium and seeing a protein of the predicted sequence emerge. We are inserting an artificial signal into the cortical circuitry and seeing a predicted behavior emerge. The opportunity for this kind of experiment is rare in systems neuroscience, but the result is most important because it confirms that the "facts" provided by single unit studies can indeed yield meaningful insight into the biological basis of behavior and cognition.

MG: The correlation of single neuron responses and psychophysical performance is fascinating but also a little bewildering. Surely lesioning a single neuron or small set of neurons would yield an animal still able to carry out the task in normal fashion. Does this argue against the sort of Barlowian view that single neurons make decisions concerning perceptual events?

WTN: I'm glad you asked that question, because many people seem to be confused about our position on this issue. Your question actually goes to the heart of the modeling efforts that Mike Shadlen, Ken Britten, Tony Movshon, and I have been involved in over the last couple of years. At first, the correlation of single neuron responses with performance pushes one toward Barlow's view that single neurons themselves, being optimally tuned detectors for certain classes of stimuli, are the critical signaling units that govern performance. Like you, however, I have difficulty believing that destruction of a single neuron could ever impair performance significantly. If this intuition is correct, the information carried by single neurons must be redundant to some extent. The important questions are: (1) how redundant, (2) how are the partially redundant signals pooled to inform psychophysical decisions, and (3) what are the key factors that limit the quality of performance emerging from the pooling process? To explore these issues, we developed a statistical model that accepts neuronal inputs like those we actually recorded in MT and produces decisions concerning the direction of motion for each stimulus presentation. In essence, the model allows us to mimic entire physiological/psychophysical experiments on the computer, and to identify conditions under which we can obtain the same relationships between physiological responses and performance that we observe experimentally.

Without going into onerous detail, we have great difficulty accounting for all of our experimental observations with small pools of input neurons (i.e., < 50). Thus we are tilting even farther away from optimal detector ideas in favor of models involving more extensive pooling. We can reproduce our experimental observations for large pools of simulated MT neurons under three key conditions: (1) the activity of neurons in the input pool is weakly correlated, (2) the psychophysical decision is influenced not only by optimally activated MT neurons, but also by neurons less sensitive than those we studied, and (3) noise sources exist at the pooling stage. The first condition has been confirmed experimentally by Ehud Zohary in our lab (*Nature* 370: 140), and we based the simulations in part on his measurements of correlated activity in MT. The second condition is a matter of conjecture, but is certainly reasonable. The third condition must be true if the pooling is performed by real neurons in the brain rather than by a digital computer.

One of the most interesting insights to emerge from the simulations is that very weak correlation among the input neurons places fundamental limits on the benefits of signal averaging within the nervous system. In our simulations, psychophysical sensitivity asymptotes as the size of the input pool reaches 50–100 neurons. The key intuition here is that noise which is common to all neurons in the pool (by virtue, perhaps, of common input from other neural structures) can never be averaged out. Thus pools consisting of thousands of input neurons would not improve performance appreciably beyond the level supported by 100 neurons. In a sense, then, the issue of numbers of neurons becomes somewhat defused. One might still search for models that could reconcile our data with *very* small numbers of neurons (i.e., < 50), but in terms of the benefits endowed by signal averaging, size appears irrelevant after the pool exceeds 100 or so neurons. In the end, this point of view need not be incompatible with Barlow's original neuron doctrine. If signals can be carried with asymptotic fidelity by small groups of 100 or so neurons, then single neurons remain a force to be reckoned with.

I should mention for interested readers that a preliminary description of our modeling results appears in *The Cognitive Neurosciences,* published by MIT Press.

MG: Is it possible that the nervous system uses more neurons than absolutely necessary for many tasks, thereby assuring behavioral competence in the face of an ever-degenerating brain?

WTN: Of course it is possible. This sort of redundancy would give the organism no advantage in the short run, however, and would presumably entail a sacrifice of potential computational power. What is the optimal trade-off between present computational power and protection against future degeneration? I have no idea, but a substantial amount of protection would be provided simply by doubling the size of a sensory pool from, say, 100 to 200 neurons. Our simulations suggest that performance would be essentially unchanged by the random loss of half of these neurons.

MG: The stimulation experiments raise many questions. Do you think the site of the effect is in MT or is it elsewhere?

WTN: This is a strange question if you think about it carefully, but it comes up over and over again. To answer the question, we must be precise about the meaning of the phrase, "site of the effect." Do we mean the site where microstimulation directly affects neuronal activity? The site where directional signals become differentially active? The site(s) where the decision is made? The site(s) where the operant response is planned? The site(s) where perception occurs (if indeed any percept accompanies microstimulation in MT)? The meaning you choose will influence the answer I give, but I am not sure that this would be a useful way for us to proceed. For me, it is more helpful to think of the monkey's performance on this task as a complex sensorimotor loop. The direction of stimulus motion is encoded implicitly in sequences of activity among retinal ganglion cells. This information is made explicit in the form of directionally selective responses in neurons of the cortical motion pathway, including MT. Directional information is "read out" of this pathway by means that are not yet known, and the intention to make a specific operant response is formed and held in register in premotor circuitry. When the "go" signal occurs, motor circuits flash into action, generating the response. In principle, we could cause identical changes in the monkey's behavior by stimulating at any of these stages if we had the right number of electrodes in the right spots, active at the right times. My point is that the behavioral changes elicited by microstimulation in MT involve a cascade of activity from MT through the central nervous system to the extra-ocular muscles. So I'm not sure that it makes sense to speak of one "site of the effect." I prefer to think of a sensorimotor, or "cognitive" loop through the brain, and of microstimulation as a tool for intervening at discrete points in the loop.

I can relate an amusing anecdote concerning this point. I once participated in a small meeting of reputable neuroscientists, and I was being circumspect as usual about the "site" of the microstimulation effect (loops, opportunities for intervention, etc.). At one point, a particularly august participant brought me to a complete halt by interrupting: "I don't understand, Bill, why don't you just say that MT is where *it* happens?" with pregnant emphasis on the *it*. The problem of course is that I still don't know what *it* was. Perception? Cognition? Consciousness? I believe that mental phenomena result from interactions among networks of neurons. The attempt to restrict any one phenomenon to a particular brain structure (even MT!) is probably misguided in the long run. On the other hand, performance of a specific cognitive task certainly consists of computations executed in parallel and in sequence within real neural pathways. It seems to me entirely possible, with current techniques, to explore the inner workings of cognition by discovering the sites in well-defined neural pathways where the results of these computations become evident, and developing testable models of how these computations are implemented. This, at any rate, is what we hope to accomplish with our motion discrimination task.

MG: Granted that the proper pattern of stimulation at any stage of the pathway can, in principle, create identical behavioral effects, would you agree that these different stimulation regimes might create entirely different internal experiences for the animal?

WTN: Absolutely. Imagine for a moment that someone did microstimulation experiments on *my* brain as I performed this direction-discrimination task. Presumably, the experimenters would have several ways of causing me to choose upward motion even when the visual stimulus contained downward motion. One way would be to stimulate early regions of my visual system in a way that mimicked precisely the pattern of neural activity evoked by an upward stimulus. At the other extreme, they could simply intervene at the last moment in my oculomotor pathways to change my operant response. Now I certainly believe that my internal experience would be vastly different under these two regimes. In the former, I would actually have seen upward motion. In the latter, I would be grossly alarmed, wondering why my brain did not produce the eye movement I intended to make.

Furthermore, I believe the nature of this internal experience *matters* for our understanding of nervous system function. In some circles, it seems fashionable to suppose that internal experience is irrelevant from a scientific point of view. If we can completely explain a sensorimotor behavior in terms of causes and their effects in central neural pathways, we have accomplished everything important and can move on to the next problem. I disagree strongly with this point of view. Even if I could explain a monkey's behavior on our task in its entirety (in neural terms), I would not be satisfied unless I knew whether microstimulation in MT actually causes the monkey to *see* motion. If we close up shop and go home before answering this question and understanding its implications, we have mined silver and left the gold lying in the tailings.

Here I must admit to a major problem, though, since the monkey's internal experience is not transparent to me. We have indirect evidence concerning the nature of the animal's experience during microstimulation of MT, but I must finally admit that I do not know whether the monkey actually sees motion when we stimulate MT. To correlate perceptual experience with neural activity at this level, I believe we will ultimately have to find ways to perform conceptually similar experiments in humans.

MG: Cognitive neuroscience loves that sentiment. But back to the monkey. In an ideal world, where you could collect any data you wanted on this task, what would the final answer look like? When would you feel that you truly have an answer to how motion is perceived?

WTN: Sorry, Mike, but I don't have a good answer to that question this year. In saying this, I do not intend to be coy or obtuse. If I could answer your question straightforwardly, the implication would be that the conceptual terrain is reasonably clear, leaving hard work and a technical breakthrough or two as the only impediments to a complete understanding of motion perception. I am not that sanguine. In most branches of cognitive neuroscience, we are confronted ultimately with the curious spectacle of our own brains trying to understand themselves at their most sophisticated levels of functioning. I have substantive doubts whether we can ever accomplish this task in a completely satisfactory manner, though I would certainly enjoy coming back briefly a couple of hundred years from now to see what progress has been made!

For the time being, then, I suspect we must feel our way toward these ambitious goals from the bottom up, letting the new light obtained at each level of inquiry hint at the questions to be asked at the next level. We do not grope blindly, however, because careful psychological study of cognition can provide a reasonably clear view of many phenomena we wish to understand.

From this perspective, the best answer I can offer to your question is a list of the issues that seem most pressing at our present level of inquiry. I have offered several already, mostly fitting under the rubric of understanding information flow through the various pathways tapped by our direction-discrimination task. The more difficult issue, ultimately, is to understand how internal mental experience is related to this flow of information within neural pathways. I have already alluded to the type of experiment that seems desirable to begin addressing this issue—stimulating functionally defined circuits within the cortex of other humans, the only subjects, perhaps, with whom we share enough mental experience to make this issue truly approachable. This endeavor would require a substantive technical breakthrough, of course, so that neural circuits could be activated with fine spatial and temporal resolution in a minimally invasive manner. Even this level of inquiry would be no panacea, however, since as many questions would likely be raised as answered. But I feel certain that the "next" generation of important questions would at least become clear at that point.

Though I am sensitive to the issue of "hard" limits to our understanding, the overall endeavor of cognitive neuroscience is grand. It is worth the dedication of a scientific career, and it certainly beats cloning another gene!

MG: Thank you.

III

Neural Basis of Memory

5

Neurons and Memory
Randy Gallistel

Randy Gallistel has been a professor in the Department of Psychology at UCLA since 1989. He received his B. A. from Stanford in 1963 and his Ph.D. from Yale in 1966. He joined the faculty of the psychology department at the University of Pennsylvania in 1966 and eventually served a term as chair of that department. His experimental research focuses on the psychophysical study of electrical self-stimulation of the brain, in the conviction that the self-stimulating rat is a nerve-memory preparation in which it should someday be possible to study the cellular and molecular bases of information storage and computation in the nervous system.

With Rochel Gelman, his wife, he co-authored The Child's Understanding of Number, *which appeared in 1978. His* The Organization of Action *appeared in 1980, followed 10 years later by* The Organization of Learning. *The latter two books aimed to establish a broad conceptual framework for understanding the neural basis of learning and motivation, which are his primary interests. He has also written extensively on animal cognition, with particular focus on the representation of space, time, and number, and the role these representations play in determining animal behavior. He was a Fellow of the Center for the Advanced Study in the Behavioral Sciences in 1984–1985, chaired the Publications Board of the Psychonomics Society, 1987–1989, and was chair of the Psychology Section of the AAAS in 1994.*

MG: This is the decade of the brain and with all the hype you would think we are minutes away from understanding almost everything. Yet most of us have the experience of becoming deeply frustrated with our profound ignorance of basic issues regarding how nervous systems get their job done. From your perspective what are some of the thorniest issues we face in the years ahead?

CRG: A fundamental issue—recognized as such by everyone—is how the nervous system stores information. I believe that real progress on this question will have to wait until behavioral scientists have established a more coherent and quantitative notion of what it is we should be looking for at the cellular level. It is more or less taken for granted by those who are trying to understand information storage at the cellular level that storing information involves changing the strengths of synaptic connections. In fact, some people think this is a truism, that it could not be false. The strength of this belief is reflected in the current enthusiasm for the idea that long-term potentiation (LTP) is the cellular basis of memory. The evidence linking LTP to memory is weak, but people think that it's the best hypothesis we've got because it's the best example we have of a somewhat enduring change in synaptic connectivity.

MG: What do you mean by a more coherent and quantitative notion of what we should be looking for?

CRG: We need to be able to give nontrivial answers to the following question: What property does LTP possess—other than lasting more than a few minutes—that we know the memory mechanism must possess? This obvious question is an embarrassment to behavioral science. It is reasonable for the neurophysiologists to ask in response: Well, what properties does the behavioral study of memory tell us the memory mechanism must have? For example, how long do memories last—hours, days, weeks, the life of the organism? Behavioral science cannot provide an answer to this simple quantitative question about memory. Most students of memory would be reluctant to venture an answer, because they are painfully aware of the many methodological problems that have prevented our answering this simple question.

MG: All right, so we cannot say how long the molecular change that mediates memory formation must endure. What quantitative properties of memory can we say must be manifest at the molecular level? Surely, there is at least one quantitative fact about memory that would be useful in testing proposed cellular and molecular mechanisms of memory?

CRG: It used to be argued that there was a narrow temporal window following the onset of one stimulus—a window on the order of half a second to one second in duration—during which the second stimulus had to occur if association formation was to occur. This assumption about the conditioning process is still widely taken for granted by researchers focusing on the neurobiology of conditioning. For example, in the November 1993 issue of *Trends in Neurosciences,* in an article entitled, "Memories are made of this," P. N. R. Usherwood writes, "The temporal relationship between the conditioned and unconditioned stimuli is of critical importance for any type of conditioning; that is, the unconditioned stimulus must follow very briefly after the conditioned stimulus" (*TINS,* 1993, *16,* 427).

Unfortunately, this is not an empirically defensible assertion about associative memory. Determining the critical interval between the conditioned stimulus (CS) and the unconditioned stimulus (US) is an unresolved problem in the associative theory of learning. In fact, the thrust of the experimental results in recent years is that there is no such thing as a critical CS-US interval. The experiments that purported to determine one forgot to control for the intertrial interval. They varied the interval between the CS and the US but they did not vary the interval from one US to the next. In most conditioning experiments, this US-US interval is determined by or proportionate to the intertrial interval. Whenever people have varied the intertrial interval in conditioning experiments, they have found that it has a huge effect on the rate of conditioning. For a given CS-US interval, the longer the intertrial interval, the fewer the trials required for conditioning. It appears, moreover, that there is no effect of the CS-US interval per se. The rate of conditioning is determined by the ratio of the CS-US interval to the US-US interval. Thus, even the supposed dependence of conditioning on temporal pairing is deeply in doubt.

Curiously, the inability of learning theorists to develop an empirically defensible specification of stimulus pairing has no observable impact on, for example, research on LTP. People are trying to show that LTP depends on temporal pairing because they think that conditioning depends on temporal pairing. They are building their theoretical castles on conceptual sand. There is no good experimental evidence that conditioning does depend on temporal pairing in the sense specified by Usherwood, which is the sense in which neurobiologists understand temporal pairing. Even *Aplysia* show background conditioning, that is, they "associate" the experimental environment with the USs that occur while they are in that environment. Often, the first US does not occur until many minutes after the animal has been placed in the experimental environment, so the notion of temporal pairing invoked by Usherwood as "of critical importance for any type of conditioning" does not apply to background conditioning. (Indeed, it is unclear what notion of temporal pairing is appropriate to the analysis of background conditioning.) But the phenomenon of background conditioning is fundamental to all modern theories of associative learning.

MG: Your answer suggests a certain skepticism about current research on the neural basis of learning and about LTP as a cellular mechanism of memory. Do you think current research on the neural basis of learning is on the wrong track? Do you think LTP will prove to be the cellular mechanism that mediates classical conditioning?

CRG: Yes, I think current research is on the wrong track and, no, I do not think LTP is likely to be an important cellular mechanism in conditioning. I think that current research on memory is directed by a fundamentally erroneous conception of what the elements of memory formation are. Neuroscientists think about learning and memory only in terms of changes in synaptic connectivity based on the temporal pairing of signals. The commitment to this conception—the belief that the associative analysis of learning must be true, at least at the cellular level—is most of what fuels the current enthusiasm for LTP.

The question neurobiologists ought to be asking is not, What is the cellular and molecular basis of association formation? Rather, they should ask, What is the cellular and molecular basis of the nervous system's ability to store and retrieve the values of variables? This is a profoundly different question. When you formulate the question that way, LTP looks like a poor candidate to be the mechanism by which the nervous system stores the values of variables, because LTP decays continuously with time. Decaying continuously with time is a disastrous property to have in the physical variable that represents the value of a computational variable. Should we imagine that the value represented changes as the LTP decays? Suppose, for example, that we imagine the magnitude of the LTP at some set of synapses specifies the temporal interval between CS onset and US onset in a rabbit eyeblink experiment. (We know the rabbit learns this temporal interval because the latency of its blink is roughly proportionate to the CS-US interval.) If we keep the rabbit out of training for some months to let the LTP decay, does the latency of the eyeblink get shorter?

MG: But in neural net theories, the values of variables are not represented by the strengths of individual synaptic connections, they are represented by the patterns of strengths across many synapses in the network. Why couldn't LTP function as the storage mechanism in a neural net?

CRG: Well, it might. In that case, the decay of LTP and hence of connection strengths with time might not pose the problem I just mentioned. However, the assumption that this is how the nervous system is able to use a decaying process to preserve the values of variables strongly constrains the form of LTP's decay. All the different synapses involved in coding a given value have to decay exponentially and with the same time constant. Otherwise, their relative strengths will change as decay progresses. Also, I would think that decaying connectivity would play havoc with the effects of training experiences spread out over time, as training always is. The current strength of a connection would be some weird combination of two quite unrelated effects. One effect is the effect of the training experiences. The other determinant of connectivity would be decay. The longer since the last update of a given connection strength, the more that strength will have decayed. I would think this would have disastrous consequences for the functioning of the net, that is, for its ability to converge on a set of weights suitable for dealing with all the different training examples.

In any event, if people thought about memory as preserving the values of variables, these would be among the first questions they would ask when a neurobiologist proposed that a continuously decaying process like LTP was the basis of memory. If anyone is asking these questions, it has not come to my attention. Instead they ask if LTP depends on temporal pairing, which is not the right question to ask.

MG: What other key questions do you think we are a long way from answering?

CRG: The question of how we should conceive of information storage in the nervous system is closely related to other fundamental but less widely recognized problems. Psychological theories are moving more and more in a computational direction. Even those who believe that the brain computes in a fundamentally different way from the way computers do think that we have to describe what the brain does in computational terms. I strongly agree. In fact, I think computational descriptions of psychological processes will prove to be a necessary intermediary in the process of linking psychological processes to their neural realization. An immediate implication of this, it seems to me, is that to understand how the nervous system mediates higher psychological functions, we must understand how it computes.

We clearly do not understand how the nervous system computes. We do not know what are the foundations of its ability to compute. We do not understand how it carries out the small set of arithmetic and logical operations that are fundamental to any computation, the operations that are part of the basic instruction set in any computer ever developed, including massively parallel computers and neural net computers. We do not, for example, understand how neurons multiply, add, and compare the values of variables.

It is generally assumed that the values of variables are represented in the nervous system in one of two ways: (1) by the frequency with which axons fire, or (2) by the resultant vector in a population of cells. In either case, it is unclear what neural mechanism enables the nervous system to combine arithmetically the values thus represented. How are two rates of firing combined to generate a rate of firing proportionate to the product or the sum of the two rates? We don't know. It is far from clear that synaptic integration provides a satisfactory realization of the addition operation, much less the multiplication operation. You can look a long time through the neurophysiological literature without finding an example of a neural circuit in which the firing rate of a postsynaptic neuron is a linear function of the firing rates of two or more presynaptic neurons over some nontrivial dynamic range (say, two orders of magnitude; 1 to 100). It is even less clear how the nervous system computes resultant vectors. And if it does compute resultant vectors, it is unclear how it multiplies the values represented by two such resultants.

Moreover, we cannot be confident that these are the only ways in which neural activity represents the values of variables. I suspect we have barely scratched the surface in determining how the nervous system represents the values of variables. Until you know how the values of variables are represented in a computational device, you can hardly proceed to ask how it combines and compares those values. If you do not know how a computational device represents the values of variables and you do not know how it adds, multiplies, and compares those variables, your understanding of that device has a long way to go.

So, in brief, other key issues are: How does the nervous system represent the values of variables? What are the elementary operations in neural computation? How are they executed? The question of information storage or memory is really subsumed in the first of these questions. The question of memory is simply the question of how the nervous system represents the value of a variable when it must preserve that value indefinitely. Both the "firing rate" mechanism and the "resultant vector" mechanism serve to represent the values of variables only transiently or on the fly, so to speak. No one knows what the long-term mechanism might be.

MG: Can you explain what you mean when you say that the value of a variable may be represented by the resultant vector in a population of firing neurons?

CRG: This idea is cropping up all over the place. Electrophysiologists have repeatedly found cells in sensory and motor structures with a broad tuning to one or more dimensions of a variable. That is, they fire to a restricted range of values. The tuning—the range of values for which firing of the cell is observed—varies from cell to cell. For example, cells in the deep layers of the superior colliculus are tuned to the directions (azimuth and elevation) of visual and auditory distal stimuli. Each cell responds only to stimuli located within a cone of directions. Different cells are tuned to different directions. But the tuning is broad, and the regions to which different cells are tuned overlap considerably. Note that direction is a vector variable, that is, a variable with more than one dimension (in this case, two dimensions, azimuth and elevation). The same thing shows up in the motor cortex, where cells are tuned to the direction of a to-be-executed arm movement, and in the hippocampus, where cells are tuned to an animal's place in the environment, and in the FM/FM area of the bat auditory cortex, where cells are tuned to the distance between the bat and the target (a scalar, that is, a one-dimensional variable), and in many, many other neural structures as well.

Because of the broad tuning with extensive overlap, any actual value of the variable to which cells are sensitive is represented by (or, at least, accompanied by) the firing of many cells in the same field. The question is, what about the activity in a population of cells with overlapping tuning curves specifies the actual value of the scalar or vector variable (e.g., the direction of the movement, or the distance of the target, or the location of the animal)? One answer for which there is increasing experimental support is that each cell in the field can be thought of as a vector pointing toward the best tuning value for that cell; the direction, distance, or location, etc. that produces the most vigorous firing of that cell. The values to which cells point may be imagined to be arrayed on the circumference of a circle (in the one-dimensional case) or the surface of a sphere (in the two-dimensional case), with the origin of all the vectors at the center of the circle or sphere. Then the firing rate of a cell may be thought of as specifying the length (magnitude) of the vector it represents. The more vigorously the cell fires, the longer its vector. In effect, the more vigorously it fires, the more insistently a cell points toward "its" value. The value specified by the ensemble of firing cells is commonly assumed to be the direction in which the resultant vector points. Mathematically, the resultant vector is obtained by summing the vectors represented by each individual cell. How the resultant vector is determined neurobiologically remains to be specified. Nonetheless, this is the first new idea about how the nervous system represents the value of a variable since the beginning of this century.

MG: To return to your critique of associative theory, why have you argued in some of your talks that the associative bond is the phlogiston of psychology?

CRG: In that talk, as in my recent book, *The Organization of Learning*, I argue that the process of association formation—as traditionally understood—is not involved in any form of learning that has been experimentally investigated, including classical and instrumental conditioning. This is such a radical argument that it is difficult to reduce it to a few words. There are two components to it.

First, there are many, many examples of learning where it seems impossible to conceptualize the underlying process in associative terms. One of my favorites is how migratory thrushes learn of the center of rotation of the night sky during the period when they are nestlings. They use their knowledge of the location of the celestial pole in the night sky to hold their southward course during the nighttime portions of their first migratory flight.

Another favorite example of a nonassociative learning phenomenon is learning your position by dead reckoning, which is a ubiquitous process in animal navigation. It is well-developed even in insects. Dead reckoning is so unlike the traditional conception of learning that many people are tempted to reject it as an instance of learning. You have to remind them that the pretheoretical definition of learning is the process (or processes!) by which we acquire knowledge. Because dead reckoning is clearly a mechanism by which the ant acquires knowledge of its position, it is a learning mechanism. Like all learning mechanisms, it computes and stores the value(s) of variables. In this case, the mechanism computes the values of the variables that represent the animal's position relative to its nest or home base. The computation is equivalent to integrating velocity with respect to time.

These examples of nonassociative learning mechanisms have led me and others to argue that there is no unitary learning process at the computational level of analysis. There are many different learning mechanisms or modules. Gould and Marler have called these different problem-specific learning mechanisms "instincts to learn." Each such mechanism has a structure that enables it to compute certain facts about the world. This specialization of computational structure renders the mechanism hopelessly ill-suited for computing other facts about the world. For that, one needs other mechanisms, with a different computational structure.

The only thing that different learning mechanisms may have in common is that they may all make use of the same set of elementary computational operations. In computer terms, they may all use the same basic instruction set. (Of course, they may not. At a time when we cannot specify the instruction set underlying any computation of any substantial complexity, we are in no position to say whether different complex computations use the same elementary computational operations.)

The other thing that all learning mechanisms must do is store and retrieve the values of variables. The bird has to store the values that represent the center of rotation of the night sky and retrieve those values when it determines what orientation to adopt with respect to whatever constellation of circumpolar stars it can see at the moment. The foraging bee must store the distance and direction of the food source and retrieve these values when it gives the dance that transmits these values to other foragers. The dead reckoning mechanism must store the values that represent the animal's current position and then add to them whenever the animal moves, because dead reckoning amounts to keeping a running sum of your displacements.

In short, the first part of the argument is that instead of having a general-purpose associative learning mechanism, what we in fact have are many problem-specific learning mechanisms. None of these problem-specific learning mechanisms operates in accord with the principles of associative learning.

MG: But what about classical conditioning, the most thoroughly studied of all learning phenomena? Surely classical conditioning is mediated by associative mechanisms.

CRG: The second component of the argument is that associative theories of conditioning are having a more and more difficult time explaining the results of classical conditioning experiments. As contemporary associative theories are modified in order to deal with the really fascinating experimental results from the last 30 years (a golden age in the experimental study of conditioning), they look less and less like the simple associative models that form the conceptual framework within which neurobiologists try to determine the cellular basis of conditioning. For example, a fundamental assumption in all contemporary theories of associative conditioning is that the strength of other associations is a determinant of the increment or decrement in strength of a given association that will occur on any given trial. How the strengths of other associations—that is, the synaptic conductances at other synapses—can determine the change in conductance produced by signal pairing at a given synapse is unclear. Moreover, as I indicated above, the idea that signal pairing is crucial to conditioning is itself ever more doubtful.

MG: But if associative theories do not explain conditioning—an experimental paradigm that was developed to study association formation—what kind of theory does?

CRG: There is much evidence that what is crucial in conditioning is that the animal learns the temporal intervals between events (CS and US onsets and offsets). The simplest evidence for this was known even to Pavlov. I alluded to it above. The simplest evidence is that in many conditioning paradigms the latency of the conditioned response roughly matches the CS-US interval. In the eyeblink paradigm, if the air puff comes a quarter-second after tone onset, the rabbit learns to blink a quarter-second after tone onset; if it comes three-quarters of a second after, the rabbit blinks after three-quarters of a second. If the shock in a conditioned emotional reaction paradigm occurs 50 seconds after tone onset, the rat is at its jumpiest 50 seconds after the tone comes on.

It is only recently, however, that we have begun to appreciate how much of classical conditioning can be explained by the assumption that the animal has learned the relevant temporal intervals—together with the assumption of a few simple but decidedly computational decision processes, which translate this knowledge into behavior. The analysis of conditioning from an interval-timing perspective throws new light on a whole range of conditioning phenomena. It explains in a very natural way the fact that the rate of conditioning depends on the ratio between the CS-US interval and the US-US interval (that is, the intertrial interval). It explains the pervasive effects of background conditioning, that is, the effect of what the animal learns about the base rate of US occurrence (the rate of occurrence in the presence of the experimental apparatus). In so doing, these interval-timing theories yield a new and more rigorous analysis of the notion of CS-US contingency, which is an important but conceptually murky aspect of the modern analysis of conditioning.

The realization that the animal in a conditioning experiment learns the CS-US interval and the US-US interval sheds new light on backward conditioning. It has recently been shown that backward pairing of the CS and the US—presenting the US before the CS—yields just as good conditioning as the more traditional forward pairing, provided one does the appropriate test of conditioning strength. Interval timing theory also brings a common conceptual framework to our understanding of the effects of delay of reward in instrumental conditioning and the effects of partial reinforcement on both instrumental and classical conditioning. The effect of partial reinforcement on rate of conditioning and trials to extinction has long proved refractory to explanation within the framework of associative theory. And from the perspective of discrete-trials associative theories, there is no apparent connection between the effects of partial reinforcement and delay of reinforcement. From the perspective of interval timing theory, on the other hand, partial reinforcement and delay of reward are essentially equivalent and can be predicted within a single conceptual framework that makes use of few or no free parameters.

It also emerges that some of the more interesting aspects of operant conditioning, such as the matching phenomenon, can be explained by interval timing assumptions.

Thus, the study of classical conditioning is leading to the same conclusion that the study of nonassociative learning mechanisms leads us to: that learning involves computing and storing the values of variables. In the case of conditioning, the crucial remembered variables are the temporal intervals between events. But this conception of conditioning is as different from the traditional associative conception as the oxygen theory is different from the phlogiston theory. If this conception prevails, then the associative bond will indeed prove to have been the phologiston of psychology.

MG: You have written about a geometric "module" in the rat brain—do you think "modules" or "faculties" are a good way of thinking about brains in general?

CRG: Definitely. A modular view of learning is implicit in my arguments about learning mechanisms as adaptive specializations or instincts to learn. I think Chomsky was right to argue that there is a module for learning language. In fact, I think he was right to call it an organ, because I think the analogy to the specialization of structure and function that we see in organs is an appropriate way to think about the specialization of structure and function we see in the various learning organs. The language organ is just one example among many. These organs within the brain are neural circuits whose structure enables them to perform one particular kind of computation. This view is the norm these days in neuroscience. I do not know of anyone advocating the kind of mass action that Lashley suggested. It seems clear that different regions of the cortex (and different nuclei in the brain stem) compute different aspects of the input. Both the electrophysiology and the psychophysics of the last 30 years lead to this conclusion. It is somewhat paradoxical that neurobiologists are strongly committed to a modular view of sensory and motor processes while at the same time they embrace a nonmodular, general-process view of learning processes.

MG: What are your views on discontinuities between humans and other animals? Most neurobiologists try to generalize from animal models to the human brain—do you think it could go the other way around, that the complex cognitive models that have been proposed for humans might also apply to nonhuman animals in some form?

CRG: Humans are mammals, with the mammalian brain plan, and they share many basic motor and perceptual capacities with many other mammals. There is therefore a strong presupposition of continuity in brain function. I think the notion of modules can help us think about both the continuities and discontinuities between human and animal brains. I assume that most of the modules in the visual cortex are the same in macaque monkeys and humans—partly because the psychophysics of macaque vision so far look almost identical to the psychophysics of human vision. Thus, I think we can use the findings regarding the neural basis of, say, large-field motion perception in the macaque to make plausible inferences about the neural basis of this same process in humans. On the other hand, we may never be able to study the neural basis of language perception in animals for the same reason that you cannot use a mammal to study the neural basis of polarization perception—mammals do not perceive polarization (whereas insects and, perhaps, some nonmammalian vertebrates do).

My comments on the computational nature of learning mechanisms should make it clear that the kinds of computationally complex models that have become common in human psychology are beginning to appear in animal psychology. Gibbon's scalar timing theory, which is at the heart of the interval-timing analyses of conditioning that I mentioned above, is an example. The assumption that there are computationally complex processes in animal brains more or less defines the emerging field of animal cognition. However, the ethologists, who came to the study of learning via the study of the habits of animals rather than via the philosophy of mind, have long entertained computationally complex models of learning mechanisms in animals.

Of course, the notion of computational complexity is a vague one. Dead reckoning (in essence, the integration of velocity with respect to time) strikes most undergraduates as a startlingly complex computation for an ant brain to perform. However, quite simple physical devices can realize this computation. Sun compass navigation (taking compass directions from the position of the sun), which is a ubiquitous navigational mechanism in both insects and birds, is so complex that one hesitates to try to describe it in a serious way to an undergraduate class. You have to explain what an ephemeris function is, and so on. But ethologists, who have grown used to thinking about animal navigation in terms of these experimentally well-established mechanisms, do not think of them as all that complex.

The ethologists discovered both of these learning mechanisms, just as they did other adaptively specialized learning mechanisms, such as song learning and learning the position of the celestial pole in the night sky. So computationally complex mechanisms in animals are entering people's thinking about animal behavior from two quite different directions— from human cognitive psychology and from ethology. That computationally complex ways of thinking about animal learning should enter psychology from ethology—the home of the instinct concept—is something of an irony. However, as Gould and Marler have argued, these computationally complex specialized learning mechanisms may be thought of as instincts to learn. When they make this argument, they link up with Chomsky's argument about the foundations of language learning. He argues in effect that language learning in humans is an instinct. Like most instincts, it will prevail given anything but extremely hostile environments. A bird's gotta learn what a bird's gotta learn, and ditto for humans.

Learning is made possible in animals, both human and otherwise, by computationally complex task-specific learning modules. To understand these modules neurobiologically, we are going to have to understand how neural tissue represents the values of variables, how it stores and retrieves those values, and how it implements the presumably small set of basic computational operations, such as addition and multiplication, on which all the modules depend. At the moment, we are not close to understanding any of these things. That's why behavioral neuroscience is so interesting. The most important insights lie ahead of us, not behind us.

6

Human Memory
Endel Tulving

Endel Tulving is Tanenbaum Chair in Cognitive Neuroscience at Rotman Research Institute of Baycrest Centre, University of Toronto, and Distinguished Research Professor of Neuroscience and Psychology at University of California, Davis. He was born in 1927 in Estonia and came to Canada in 1949. He did his undergraduate work at the University of Toronto and graduate work at Harvard. Throughout his professional career he has studied human memory. His discoveries and the concepts he has introduced to the field include subjective organization, input and output interference, the distinction between availability and accessibility of stored information, retrieval cue, cue-dependent forgetting, Tulving-Colotla measure of primary memory, recognition failure of recallable words and names, Tulving-Wiseman function of the relation between recognition and cued recall, encoding specificity, synergistic ecphory, encoding/retrieval interaction, the distinction between episodic and semantic memory, the GAPS model of episodic memory, stochastic independence between priming and episodic memory measures, the distinction between noetic and autonoetic consciousness, the HERA model of encoding/retrieval asymmetry of the frontal lobes, and the novelty/encoding hypothesis.

MG: Let us begin at the macro-level, human memory. What does it mean to have a theory of human memory? Or, put differently, what must a theory of human memory contain for it to reflect the known complexity of the process?

ET: I trust that you are talking about theories *about* human memory rather than theories *of* memory as such. A theory of memory would be something like a theory of light, or a theory of evolution, that tells you what it (light, evolution) is, and how its phenomena must be what they are because of what the theory says they should be, or how it is perfectly sensible that they are what they are. There have not been any theories *of* memory of this kind, and it is a reasonably safe bet that there never will be any.

Now, theories *about* memory are concerned with selected, restricted sets of phenomena of memory; they thereby escape facing the problem of complexity of memory as such. In cognitive psychology, these local theories represent, as you well know, variations on the general theme of cognition as information processing. So, memory is thought of as consisting of the processes of encoding, storing, and retrieving information, and each of these processes consists of subprocesses. Phenomena of memory are explained in terms of the characteristics of these processes, and their interactions.

As to the second part of your question, a theory of something is an explanation of that something, and to explain something means different things to different people. Some think that memory will be explained—I even fear that some might claim it will be understood—when the underlying synaptic mechanisms have been identified. There are others who think that a computer program or a mathematical model can explain memory, or at least some of its phenomena. Between these extremes are other, potentially more fruitful, basic orienting attitudes. So, given these differences, you will get different suggestions as to what the theory must contain to cope with the known process.

MG: Well, we are asking you. In particular, must a cognitive theory about memory that would please you be stated in a way that could be tested by brain scientists?

ET: Sure! But an even better idea might be to demand that a cognitive theory be stated in a way that the Almighty himself could pass judgment on. The point is that an interesting cognitive theory about memory (or a cognitive theory about some interesting phenomenon of memory)—that is, *behavior* or *experience* that can be classified under the rubric—is utterly beyond the pale of most methods and techniques of today's brain science. Things may change tomorrow, of course, and then we may want to include physiological or even physical reality as a criterion for evaluating cognitive theories, but right now the insistence (you said "must it be?") on it would bring about a quick demise of cognitive theories of memory.

Look, we have great difficulties making *psychological* sense of many things we observe about memory, that is, just making up plausible, reasonably economical, and internally consistent stories about those phenomena that have caught the intellectual fancy of a particular generation of practitioners. If we had to start worrying about whether a favorite theory of ours is really true, that is, how Mother Nature planned it all, or if we began expecting that people in some other branch of the science of memory do so, we and they would probably freeze in thought instantly.

MG: When people commonly think of memories, of recalling past experience, they imagine the information is somehow recorded in a particular site in the brain. Is there anything wrong with that folk notion, the same notion most brain scientists believe to be true? Or jumping ahead, what are the five facts of memory that brain scientists ought to be considering as they pursue the physical dimensions of this problem?

ET: Let me just answer the first part of the question. We will see later whether we get around to the second part.

There is nothing wrong *in principle* with the idea that the information that is necessary for remembering something is recorded in a particular site in the brain. It is almost a tautology: When an event occurs that a person perceives and subsequently remembers, some changes must occur in the brain. That is, the brain is different before and after that event, or experience, or whatever. We can call that before-after difference the engram, or the memory, trace, or representation of the event, or whatever. The engram, by definition, must be localizable somewhere in the brain. This is why the idea of the engram was scientifically respectable long before Lashley began his famous and eventually inconclusive search for it, and why it is still so.

MG: Why did you say *in principle* nothing is wrong with the idea of physical storage?

ET: I said "nothing wrong in principle," because in practice there does exist a problem, quite apart from the complexity of it all. The concept of engram, however it is labeled, has mesmerized many brain scientists into acting as if there was nothing more to the problem of memory and the brain than the engram and its characteristics including its location in the overall structure. Many of these brain scientists, like many non-scientists, do not seem to realize that the engram is an unfinished thought about memory, that it is at best only one-half the story of memory. This being so, when they concentrate on the one half and ignore the equally essential other half, they may be doing the right thing, or they may be doing the wrong thing. It is difficult to tell in advance. I wish someone would tell me whether they are unaware of the other half, whether they are preoccupied with the engram out of sheer inertia, or whether they have reflected deeply on the matter and deliberately decided that identification of storage sites of memories is the number one priority, for such and such compelling reasons.

MG: By the "other half" you presumably mean retrieval? Storage of information, or engram, is one half, you say, and retrieval is the other half?

ET: Exactly, although I hope you realize that talking about two "halves" means simplifying the matter greatly. Also, talking about the two halves misses the most important feature of each, namely, that neither can work separately—that storage and retrieval processes receive their "identity" from the interaction between them.

A biological memory system differs from a mere physical information-storage device by virtue of the system's inherent capability of using the information in the service of its own survival, which, we are told, is any biological system's first priority. The Library of Congress, a piece of videotape, a Cray supercomputer, and many other devices that store information could not care less about their own survival. So anyone who is interested in memory, but looks only at the storage side of things, is essentially ignoring the fundamental distinction between dead and living storage systems, that is, ignoring the essence of *biological* memory.

MG: What do cognitive psychologists know about storage and retrieval that makes the distinction so crucial as you seem to be implying?

ET: Cognitive psychologists discovered retrieval and figured out how to separate it analytically and experimentally from storage in the 1960s. The predecessor of memory research in experimental psychology was verbal learning, the study of learning and retention of verbal materials. Its pre-theoretical thinking was greatly inspired by conditioning. It, too, suffered from the preoccupation with storage, although the concept was then labeled "association." The interesting thing is that students of verbal learning were unaware of their storage bias, for the simple reason that the distinction between storage and retrieval had not yet been made: You cannot be aware of something that does not exist. I should mention parenthetically that for the first six years or so of my post-doctoral life I too was one of those happy verbal learners who did not lose any sleep over the storage-retrieval distinction. When things changed, the field of verbal learning essentially died.

It would not be difficult to argue that the "discovery" of retrieval *processes* permanently revolutionized the field of memory research in cognitive psychology. And yet, as I see things, that revolution has not yet reached brain scientists. I have seen little evidence that retrieval processes occupy their thoughts or shape their activities.

MG: Brain scientists ignore the larger question because they do not have any idea how to study the issue from a neural systems point of view. The synapse is where the light is shining, which is to say it is something that can be studied. Also, at a superficial level, it makes sense that information storage ought to reflect structural and physiological changes at the synapse. Yet no one thinks memories are stored at synapse, that is, if you push them on it. So, that suggests brain scientists would be well served to have the problem properly characterized. Any comments?

ET: I hope you are not implying that you or I should tell the brain scientists what their proper problems are! Such an action would generate only heat and absolutely no light.

Surely they are doing the best they can. Besides, there is nothing wrong with studying what is possible to study, and not worrying about what is not; the same venerable principle holds in all sciences. And what is possible to study at a given time depends to a large extent on the amount of relevant knowledge that has already accumulated.

Having said that, let me nevertheless offer a possibly pertinent thought. Of course memories are not stored at synapses. But I think it is useful to contemplate the possibility that they are not stored anywhere else in the brain either. The whole issue of where or, more important, how memories are stored in the brain may turn out to be an incorrect formulation of the problem, despite its seductively enticing allure. And the source of such an incorrect formulation may lie in the single-minded preoccupation with the storage, or the engram, and sometimes even *identification* of storage with memory. This preoccupation with the physical changes that follow from an experience that can be remembered seems to be accompanied by a rather conspicuous neglect of retrieval processes.

MG: So, you are not telling brain scientists what their proper problems are, but you are telling them where they seem to be missing the boat?

ET: I am just telling you about my casual, and possibly quite incorrect, impressions about the brain science side of things in memory research. If a brain scientist's curiosity is piqued about this vague talk about the crucial distinction between storage and retrieval, and if he then decides to do something about it, it is his right and privilege. I would not want to prescribe research problems for people in a different discipline any more than I would care about such prescriptions coming from them.

But I cannot deny that I would be pleased to see the whole issue openly discussed, and at least some brain scientists experimenting with formulations that place the emphasis on the nature of brain activity that subserves or produces the kind of mental *activity* that is identified with memory in cognitive psychology.

MG: And synaptic mechanisms are not part of that activity? Surely those mechanisms are involved, and perhaps even determine, storage?

ET: *The key process of memory is retrieval.* The storage or engram alone, in the absence of retrieval, is no better than no storage and no engram at all. If you know something, or if you have stored information about an event from the distant past, and never use that information, never think of it, your brain is functionally equivalent to that of an otherwise identical brain that does not contain that information. And it is but a small step from this idea of functional equivalence to the idea of structural equivalence: An engram does not exist independently of retrieval, that is, a brain "containing" a nonretrieved engram is structurally equivalent to an otherwise identical brain that does not contain that particular engram.

MG: Now you are losing me. Earlier you said the engram exists, it is physical, and it is localized, and now you are saying it does not exist? Is this a new version of one of those famous Zeno's paradoxes?

ET: It may sound like a paradox, but it is not. A physical engram exists, but it cannot be identified as an engram by any physical means, it can be identified only through its biological-psychological action, through the retrieval process.

As a scientist I am compelled to the conclusion—not postulation, not assumption, but conclusion—that there must exist certain physical-chemical changes in the nervous tissue that correspond to the storage of information, or to the engram, changes that constitute one of the necessary conditions of remembering. (The alternative stance, that it may be possible for any behavior or any thought to occur independently of physical changes in the nervous system, as all your good readers know, is sheer mysticism.) However, if the engram is a kind of an entity that manifests itself only in activity, or retrieval, then we might conjecture that the physical changes resulting from an experience do not exist as an engram in the absence of that activity. And we can also imagine that the engram, *qua engram,* is not detectable in its quiescent state, that is, in the absence of retrieval, with any physical technique.

Let me give you a very simple and in many ways inadequate analogy that illustrates, or at least hints at, the kind of a situation we have on our hands.

Wind is the movement of air molecules. To create something that we identify as wind, two necessary conditions must be satisfied: (1) the presence of the air molecules in sufficient quantity and density, and (2) the operation of some source of energy that sets the molecules in more-or-less coordinated motion of sufficient velocity. Now think of an analogy with memory: (1) the blowing wind is the brain activity that subserves the experience of remembering, (2) the air molecules constitute the physical substrate of the activity, the engram, and (3) the energizing force is the retrieval cue that "activates" or "ecphorizes" the engram. Thus, wind is particles and energy; remembering is engram and retrieval. In this analogy, the relation between the experience of remembering and the engram is the same as the relation between the wind and air molecules: the second member of each pair is a necessary condition of the first.

Now, what would you think of a sage who decides to identify the physical substrate, the engram, of the wind, and starts searching for it, assuming it to be a special entity of some kind, an entity different from other like entities that do not produce wind? Since no specifically identifiable engram in fact exists—the air molecules that can be set in motion do not differ from those that never are set in motion our sage is going to be spending a lot of time on his chosen problem, unaware that the problem is created by his ownself, by his initial presupposition, rather than by nature.

The brain scientist who is looking for a special change at the synapse, one that results from some experience, one that represents or stands for memory, and one that is different from the synaptic activity that subserves other kinds of behavior or cognition, or other kinds of physiological activity altogether, takes the risk of being terribly frustrated because, by looking for something that in fact does not exist independently of something else, he is doomed to failure, regardless of how hard he tries and how long he persists. He will have become a victim of the second of the two kinds of obstacles that lie in the path of all explorers of nature—those placed there by nature and those placed there by man.

MG: You may have just captured a brain scientist's worst nightmare. But are you simply thinking of alternatives here or is your view motivated by the consideration of some body of data? One can certainly view much of the neurobiology of synaptic change as of interest such as the work of LTP (long-term potentiation) and the fierce debate over whether or not such phenomena are pre- or postsynaptic in nature. Yet one can also observe whatever it is; there is no demonstration it has anything to do with psychological memory. Is it this kind of thing that concerns you and finds you playing with alternative formulations of the problem or is your view driven from psychological data? Alternatively, is it driven by a hunch on the nature of the problem?

ET: Remember, I am a cognitive psychologist. I deal with cognitive data, revealed through behavior. I cannot get as thrilled about LTP, or the issue of presynaptic versus post-synaptic protein synthesis as do neurobiologists, for the same reason that they do not get as thrilled about the intricacies of presemantic perceptual priming as I do: We lack the requisite background knowledge to appreciate each other's excitements. A friend of mine who is closer to the synapses than I am tells me, however, that the eventual outcome of the battle of pre- versus postsynaptic processes will have important practical consequences for problems such as drug addiction and its treatment. I believe him.

But you asked about the speculations I have just shared with you. Is it a hunch, an expression of a desire for an alternative or is it suggested by data? I would say, all of the above. It is an alternative *suggested* by the outcomes of many cognitive psychology experiments on recall and recognition.

The experiments that are particularly relevant to the issue have been done under the general rubric of encoding specificity or encoding retrieval interactions. In these experiments, the identity of the to-be-remembered items is held constant, encoding conditions are manipulated (thereby creating different engrams of physically identical items), and then these engrams are probed under different retrieval conditions. Actually, only the retrieval component of this paradigm is necessary to make my point; systematically varying encoding conditions would just add some bells and whistles to the tale.

Since what I have just said may not make total sense to all of your readers, let me try to illustrate it with a simple, concrete example. Imagine that you are the subject in one of my experiments, and that you see a *pair* of words, say LADY and QUEEN. I am telling you to make sure that you remember having seen the word QUEEN in the experiment, and that I am going to test you for it. (I should mention parenthetically that the pair of words is usually presented as a part of a larger collection, but for the purposes of our story that fact is irrelevant. I should also mention that the particular words that I am testing you with, of course, are also irrelevant. Indeed the to-be-remembered items need not be single words. The item you are asked to remember might be a unique name of a well-known character, such as GEORGE WASHINGTON or FLORENCE NIGHTINGALE. The outcome of the experiment is the same.)

Anyhow, after a while I ask you: Did you see the word QUEEN in the list that you studied? With a certain probability you say "yes," and with a certain probability you say "no." If you say "yes," I know that, because the retrieval cue that I gave you was an effective probe and the engram responded to it, the engram created at study must have existed at test. If you say no, I cannot say anything very much about the engram. It may have not been created at all, it may have been lost while other things were going on, or it may still exist but the retrieval cue I provided happened to be an inappropriate or wrong probe. So, to clarify the uncertain situation I ask you another question: What word went with the word LADY in the list that you studied? And with a certain probability, you now say, QUEEN! Thus, you cannot *recognize* (identify as previously seen in the experiment) the word you were supposed to study and to remember, and yet you can *recall* (produce) it to another cue.

What these and many other similar kinds of data tell us is that in a fixed encoding situation that has produced a fixed engram of a particular event (such as seeing two familiar words in a particular place at a particular time), whether the engram responds to the probe depends on the probe. One and the same engram responds to some probes and not others. In our example the interesting thing is that it does *not* respond to the probe that is most like the specified target item, but *does* respond to a related item.

MG: Hold it for a second! How is it possible for me to recall something that I do not recognize? Or, in terms of your engram story, why should the engram of the word I have seen and am now trying to remember fail me when I try to retrieve it with a virtual copy of the original, and yet respond satisfactorily if I can go after the stored information with a cue different from the item I am trying to recover?

ET: Well, until about twenty years ago everybody (including the proverbial man in the street, the brain scientist, and the cognitive psychologist) *knew* that such a happening (recall but no recognition) was indeed not possible. Yet today it is not only possible—first year psychology students who learn about it find it perfectly reasonable when they are told what is going on—we also have a pretty good idea what is happening in the situation that I just described.

This particular outcome does not happen all the time, as I said, but only with a certain probability. In fact, the conditional probability that a studied item that can be recalled to a related cue cannot be recognized when presented by itself varies systematically from very low (near zero) to very high (unity). We know a fair amount about such systematic variability. But that is another story.

MG: You do not think this other story is relevant here?

ET: Not really, and certainly not directly. So, let me return to the implications of the fact that one and the same engram responds to (or recognizes if you wish) some probes but not others. In our experiment, we used the most natural kind of probe possible: another complex stimulus input into the system. Johannes Müller would have said, the most adequate stimulus. The effectiveness of this kind of probe, or cue, has been shaped by evolution over the eons. And we find that the engram is highly specific: it is identified, "located," or activated (I sometimes use the term "ecphorized") by one likely-looking *natural* cue and not another.

Now the point I want to make in this connection is this: If a given engram cannot be identified by *some* of the most natural (i.e., biological) probes, although it can by others, how reasonable is it to expect that you could identify it using some artificial (i.e., physical) probe or detection device? What would you be looking for, and how would you know what it is that you have identified, in the absence of retrieval? Even if you could somehow identify the total pattern of physical/chemical aftereffects of an experienced event, in all of its intricate and elaborate detail and full-blown complexity, you would have no way of knowing or predicting what kind of a memory (in the sense of experience) that engram is going to produce: *that* depends on the retrieval process, and that process has not yet occurred. Aftereffects of a stimulus event do not constitute an engram. The engram consists of those components of the aftereffects that are ecphorized in the process of retrieval. This is why I suggest that it might be useful to contemplate the possibility that the engram does not exist as an identifiable entity in the absence of retrieval, although it exists as a physically unidentifiable component of the aftereffect of the stimulus event and as a necessary condition of the biological-psychological act of remembering.

MG: So what does it mean to study the synaptic mechanism of memory? How can the brain scientist distinguish between what you call aftereffects of an event and the engram, that is, the *specific* aftereffects that are "ecphorizable" in retrieval and thereby, but you say only thereby, determine whether and what the person remembers of the event?

ET: This is the sixty-four-million-dollar question. I suggest you go and ask a brain scientist who studies synaptic mechanisms of memory. All I am doing is suggesting that there may be a rather basic problem here, a kind of an unwarranted pretheoretical assumption, and that the problem does seem to require explicit thought. The brain scientist may be able to identify the aftereffects of an event, and he may even be even able to tell the difference between the aftereffects of Event A and Event B. If he studies the synaptic mechanisms that define, or are involved in, these aftereffects for their own sake, and does not worry what those aftereffects are good for, or whether they have anything to do with specific memories, that is, if he is willing to concede the possibility that he may be studying something other than a component of memory, then there is no problem. The problem arises when the aftereffects are called memory.

I am arguing, at the level of behavior and cognition, and on the basis of observed facts, that the engram does not exist as a component of memory, independently of retrieval. And I have a problem in that I cannot think of any reason why the same elementary proposition does not hold equally well at the level of physical happenings in the brain. Remember that when I talk about behavior and cognition, I am also talking about the brain. The mind is only an expression of the brain, at a different level, but nevertheless an expression. Whatever the mind can do, the brain can do better; and whatever the mind does do, the brain must have done, too, in its own way.

MG: But could it be the case that you are being too generous about what is being studied within brain science? Accepting the general concept of storage is one thing. Suggesting, however, that examining how synapses might change to reflect storage mechanisms is quite another. That, too, is a strong claim for the brain scientist to make given what everyone assumes to be the case, namely that storage is somehow a distributed process. At another level, however, the storage metaphor suggests specific memories ought to be lost with brain damage in the storage areas. Is that how you would characterize what happens following brain damage?

ET: It is not only useful but important to distinguish between the storage metaphor, on the one hand, and the idea of the physical indeterminacy of the engram, on the other. The concept of storage is a logical necessity, even if its particular formulation and the terminology one uses are necessarily quite flexible. The data from the studies of brain damage are very clear, too, in suggesting that engrams of particular *kinds* of information at least are localized in the brain, even if the localization involves distributed information. Particular lesions do produce particular deficits in memory. It is not always clear that the deficits are caused by the damage to the areas in which the information is stored—an obvious alternative hypothesis is one of disconnection between the areas concerned with storage and those concerned with retrieval— but there is little question about the *specificity* of the loss, at some level.

All this is reasonably clear. Now, to get from these data to the idea that even particular facts that we know, or particular events that we recollect, have distinct engrams requires a bit of extrapolation, although nothing in excess of the kind that is normal in scientific thinking. The problem is that the lesions that neuropsychologists and other cognitive neuroscientists have dealt with so far have almost invariably been massive. We can well imagine that one day in the future it will be possible to produce a highly circumscribed lesion, perhaps a reversible one, that has a single consequence—say, of the person not knowing anymore what a strawberry is—without any other effects whatsoever. If so, we will have obtained strong evidence of what we now can only assume, namely that engrams even of single concepts or experiences exist, that they are real (physical), that they are specific, localized, and that they represent an essential component of the memory process. But these facts would not change the basic argument I have offered here: The "strawberry engram" will have been identified by inference from the observed failure of *retrieval*.

MG: So you are saying, or at least implying, that this apparent paradox between biological determinacy and physical indeterminacy of engrams comes about because of a basic conflict, or incompatibility, between biological and physical approaches? That while the engram is all those things you said—real, specific, localizable, and so on—by biological criteria, or in terms of the biological procedures (and I'm willing to lump together biology and psychology for the present purposes, as you have been doing), it is none of those things by physical criteria, in terms of physical procedures?

ET: Precisely. This seems to be in the basic nature of things. Although I would not characterize the relation between the two kinds of approach as one of conflict or incompatibility. It is rather one of dealing with *different aspects,* or different facets, of one and the same thing. And there is nothing wrong with that, of course. Indeed, it is the only way that biological science has progressed: through examining and trying to understand objects and happenings in the world from different perspectives. There need be no conflict, as long as we understand that brain scientists who study memory by studying (physical) changes at the synapse, and, say, cognitive psychologists who study memory as "synergistic ecphory" (as a joint product of storage and retrieval *processes*), have a common object of interest, and that they are simply focusing on different aspects or facets of that common object. The approach of cognitive psychology and the approach of neurobiology are *complementary,* and there is no problem whatever. The problem arises only if one assumes that the physical approach is the only one, or the most essential one, or the fundamental one, that is, the old die-hard reductionist position. Remembering is a completely emergent, biological-psychological process of the brain. Our little chat has turned out to be an examination of the implications of such a conceptualization of memory for the study of its physical basis.

MG: Well, we are almost done. Any final, parting words you want to leave with your readers?

ET: Yes. Students of memory of the scientific world, unite in the study of the myriad aspects of the essence of biological memory, unite in the study of the interaction between the processes of storage and retrieval!

IV

Language

7

Evolutionary Perspectives
Steven Pinker

Steven Pinker is a professor in the Department of Brain and Cognitive Sciences at MIT, and director of its McDonnell-Pew Center for Cognitive Neuroscience. He received his B. A. from McGill University in 1976 and his Ph.D. from Harvard University in 1979, both in experimental psychology, and taught at Harvard and Stanford before joining the faculty of MIT in 1982.

He has done research in visual cognition and the psychology of language, and is the author of Language Learnability and Language Development *(1984/1996),* Learnability and cognition *(1989), and* The Language Instinct *(1994). His newest book,* How the Mind Works, *is due out in 1997.*

He was the recipient of the Early Career Award in 1984, the Boyd McCandless Award in 1986, and the William James Book Prize in 1995 from the American Psychological Association, a Graduate Teaching Award from MIT in 1986, and the Troland Research Award from the National Academy of Sciences in 1993.

MG: You have written a new book about the nature of human language for a general audience. Tell us what you want to communicate in *The Language Instinct?*

SP: The book is about all aspects of human language. One thing I wanted to do was to answer the kinds of questions I get asked when I tell people I study language, such as, are there really pockets of the Ozarks where people speak Elizabethan English? What language would a child speak if he were raised by wolves? What's going on when religious people "speak in tongues?" Why can't computers take dictation? Why does no one know the plural of "Walkman"? Why is English spelling so deranged? What's the scoop about the search for the mother of all languages?

But my main goal was to try to unify the study of language under a key idea: that language is an evolutionary adaptation, like echolocation in bats or the elephant's trunk. This may seem like a boring observation, but it buys a lot. It allows for a vertically integrated science of language, where everything from genes and neural networks to Orwell and dudespeak can be fit into a consistent framework. And a lot of controversies just disappear, such as whether syntactic form or semantic function is more important, or whether there would be some evolutionary paradox if humans turned out to be the only species with language. After all, no one gets upset at the idea that the elephant's trunk is both structured and useful, or that it is complex but found in only one species.

Also, treating language as a biological adaptation overturns many folk theories that pervade modern intellectual life. The books on language that you will find at your local B. Dalton all treat language as some obscure body of lore, like how to use "hopefully" correctly or the correct term for a collection of larks, something that has to be carefully passed on by English teachers and "language mavens" (who are mostly quacks, by the way). I try to show that the complexity of language really comes from the minds of ordinary children and Joe Six-packs; the rules of the schoolmarm are just minor little decorations. Also, the general picture of the human mind that you find in books and magazines—basically the blank slate, together with the concession that of course heredity and environment are inseparably, interconnectedly, intertwiningly intermingled—turns out to be woefully lame. I think that with what we now know about language, we can do better.

MG: Well, some might read you as saying that language is innate and Chomsky made that point in 1959 with his review of Skinner's "Verbal Behavior." Before going into details, how does your MIT view differ from other MIT views?

SP: Obviously, some of the key ideas in the book come from Chomsky—that there is an innate neural system dedicated to language; that his system uses a discrete combinatorial code, or grammar, to map between sound and meaning; that this code manipulates data structures that are dedicated to language and not reducible to perception, articulation, or concepts. But there are also some differences in style and substance. Chomsky's arguments for the innateness of language are based on technical analyses of word and sentence structure, together with some perfunctory remarks on universality and acquisition. I think converging evidence is crucial, and try to summarize the facts on children's development, cross-linguistic surveys, genetic language disorders, and so on.

In that sense the book is more in the tradition of George Miller and Eric Lenneberg than Chomsky. And there is one substantive difference: I argue that language is an adaptation, a product of natural selection, and hence has parts that are designed for specific functions involved in communication. Chomsky is agnostic-to-hostile about natural selection and its applicability to language. He suspects that the language faculty could have come about as an accidental product of the way the laws of physics act on the developing brain.

He has even suggested that grammar appears to have been designed for beauty, not for usefulness.

MG: Is that a way of saying that Chomsky has not really thought about how language could have developed from a biological (evolutionary) point of view? It would seem he simply observed it must be established through genetic mechanisms and moved on to other matters.

SP: The vast majority of cognitive scientists and neuroscientists have not really thought about the evolution of the brain, but I don't think that is true of Chomsky; he has thought about evolution a great deal. But he is not familiar with mainstream evolutionary biology. His views are more in the tradition of the many physicists who suspect that the theory of natural selection is somehow vacuous and circular, or that the mechanism is too klugey and random to create interesting biological systems. Their esthetic is that biological structures should somehow follow deductively from general laws and principles, like the growth of crystals.

MG: Evolutionary theory does suggest the brain is a kluge, a collection of ad hoc systems that somehow get the job done. Does your account of language, driven as it is from an evolutionary perspective, document and identify various language operations as a collection of adaptations that has accumulated over time? Chomskyans talk about the language organ as an entity that suddenly appears on the scene (in the brain). Does your analysis suggest this first approximation is insufficient in light of what is now known about language organization?

SP: The point about biological systems being collections of kluges has been a bit overdone by psychologists. If you look at many biological systems you see astoundingly sophisticated engineering, the eye being the most famous example, but with a few kluges (like the retina being installed backward) that reveal their origin as the result of selection of random small changes from an ancestral form. I think in language we certainly see signs of engineering to carry out a function. Syntax and morphology are codes that map multi-dimensional semantic data structures onto strings of symbols that can be transmitted through a serial interface. Phonology allows a finite number of sound units to be rearranged to form an open-ended set of words, and phonetics compresses the units into a signal that transmits them at a rate that exceeds the resolving power of the ear.

And, as you would expect, there are oddities and quirks that suggest that language was not designed deliberately or from scratch. The descended larynx is the obvious physiological example (good for making speech sounds at the cost of making us more likely to choke on food). At the computational level, you find examples of seemingly needless redundancy, like the fact that certain information can be conveyed either by rote memorizing lexical items or by composing structures with grammatical rules, giving us the contrast between regular and irregular forms (*take–took* versus *bake–baked*) and the resulting grammatical mayhem. The verb and preposition system seem to have been designed to convey spatial and force-dynamic information, so we have to resort to motion metaphors when talking about abstract information such as state changes (e.g., *Sam went from being sick to being well*). And no one knows how to talk about something possessed by two people (*Rob and my mother? Rob and me's mother? Rob's and my mother?*).

Regarding language appearing all at once—I don't think Chomsky has made that claim, though Derek Bickerton has suggested that it appeared in two stages. It strikes me as unlikely, for standard evolutionary reasons. If language is a complex system involving many finely interacting parts that collectively do something interesting (as Chomsky himself has shown) then by the laws of probability you would not expect one random mutation to give some fortunate ancestor all of the necessary neural modifications in one thunderclap. I also think there is evidence from neuroscience and genetics that speaks against language emerging as an automatic physical by-product of some more global development such as a large brain (which is something Chomsky has conjectured as a possibility). Across normal variation and pathology you see big differences in brain size, shape, and global organization that can coexist with intact language. This suggests that it is a certain wiring of the microcircuitry that is essential. Also, in cases of genetically transmitted specific language impairment, you don't find language wiped out entirely, but different components affected to different extents. If a single lucky genetic change had given us language, it should be possible for a mutation in that gene to wipe language out entirely, but one never sees that.

MG: Hmm, sounds like a good topic for someone working on gene knockout to consider. But let's switch gears. Sitting majestically on the other side of the biologic interpretation of language acquisition are those that feel language is learned and built up through associations. Even though Chomsky seemed to have devoured Skinner's early analysis of language along these lines, there are modern reincarnations of the environmentalist views. Neurocomputationalists have any number of algorithms that they feel can learn and handle language learning. Ever since Rosenberg and Sejnowski demonstrated that a simple neural net could read, the field has blossomed with claims. How do you see it?

SP: I feel that a lot of the work in artificial "neural networks" is based more on eighteenth-century notions of learning—mainly associative pairing and generalization by similarity—than on any systematic empirical study of what organisms' brains are computing. Randy Gallistel has made this point in reviewing the remarkable computational abilities of various animals in domains such as navigation and the perception of time and number, none of which has any need for the classical associative bond. I think his critique carries over to language (because I think psycholinguistics is a branch of ethology).

I don't think the interesting issue is whether such-and-such a class of model is capable of learning X given a suitable training regimen. That's a mathematical point, not a scientific one, and there is a consensus that most of the commonly discussed artificial neural networks can be designed either with Turing power or as universal function approximators. The interesting question is empirical: how, in fact, does the neural circuitry underlying language (or any other mental ability) work? To answer that you can't just wire up any old model, train the daylights out of it, and declare victory; you have to check if the wiring diagram really corresponds to the plausible innate organization of the creature, and whether the training schedule plausibly corresponds to its experience. In many of the connectionist models of language, neither is done. Just take the various reading-aloud models, where the designer wires together a network designed to map from visual symbols to phonology, and the network has to learn the exact mapping. Taken literally, this is a claim that we are innately designed to read—the very ability where we are 100 percent sure that there can be no innate faculty! Similarly, neural net modelers have no compunctions about building in innate wiring to perform artificial tasks of the late twentieth-century experimental psychologist, like lexical decision. The issue is not whether there is learning or innate wiring—obviously there's both. The issue is what in fact *is* the innate wiring and learning experience.

This is especially clear to me in my own empirical work, on the linguistic computation we do when creating past tense forms such as *faxed* or *broke*. In 1986 Rumelhart and McClelland published a brilliant study of how a simple feedforward network learns these mappings. Alan Prince and I noted a number of ways in which the model behaved systematically differently from people. Many involved linguistic quirks such as the fact that people can easily inflect weird-sounding verbs such as *to out-Gorbachev,* that *wring* and ring are homophonous but have different past tense forms (and so the input to the past tense system cannot be sound alone), and that verbs formed from nouns and adjectives, such as *flied out to center field* and *ringed the city,* always take regular *-ed* even if homophonous with an irregular verb.

The response of many connectionists to our critique (not Rumelhart and McClelland themselves) was to "improve" the model by adding hacks designed to handle each one of these quirks and train the improved model with the crucial examples—amounting to the bizarre claim that the brain is specifically wired, and children are specifically taught, in such a way as to make the quirks come about! This was all meant to show that a connectionist model can, in principle, handle the phenomena, but that was never our dispute. Our point was that these quirks are by-products of some fundamental ways in which the language system is organized, and that any model of how language is implemented in the brain will have to reflect that organization. In particular, we showed that the past tense computation requires at least three things: a division into subsystems (most fundamentally, the mental dictionary and the mental grammar); some way of representing the identity of entities as distinct individuals, independent of their phonological and semantic content; and a computational operation that can concatenate variables, not just analogize. These are not particularly extravagant claims, and one can imagine all kinds of neural networks that can implement them. But the standard model of a single associative network has become such doctrine that people will go to any lengths to maintain it, even if it involves innately wiring in peculiarities of English grammar and sticking exotic cases into the training set.

MG: By yanking language learning out of the field of learning mechanisms and marking it down as one of our instincts, don't you sort of also trumpet the end of its study? After all, sex is an instinct and while people study the physiological basis for aspects of sex such as arousal, there is not much more to say about it. In short, once the descriptive work is done, and the rules are written for biologically based grammar, can't you go fishing?

SP: No, I would disagree with all those assumptions, starting with sex. There is plenty to say about the cognitive psychology of sex, as shown in the work of evolutionary psychologists such as Don Symons, David Buss, Margo Wilson, and Martin Daly. The sexual "instinct" surely involves many complex information-processing mechanisms—the psychophysics of sexual attractiveness, short-term and long-term strategies for courtship and manipulation and for evaluating and resisting such tactics, and decision rules for commitment versus desertion. And many of these mechanisms are surely specific to the domain of sex, not social relations in general—as Fran Lebowitz said, you would never choose someone as a close friend because he had a really cute nose.

One of the achievements of linguistics is to show that even if a language instinct is innate, that does not mean that we announce that language belongs to the physiologists and leave it at that. There is a huge body of ongoing research showing how detailed facts of English fall out of the computational organization of the mental grammar for English, and how the mental grammar for English falls out of the universal grammar underlying all languages. But this is technical, somewhat difficult work, and many psychologists find their eyes glazing over when, say, Chomsky starts going on about *John is too stubborn for anyone to talk to*. They read the first and last ten pages of his books, with all the exciting rhetoric about innateness, skip the actual content, and then dimly remember the claims in a bumper-sticker form ("language is innate") that seems to leave no room for anyone but the physiologists.

More generally, it's wrong to equate "instinct" and "physiology" (or "innateness" and "wiring"). Neural tissue, at the level at which a physiologist studies it, is not going to do anything that corresponds directly to interesting psychology. That is, you might discover that the geometry of a dendrite or the strength of a synapse functions in some way that corresponds to a logic gate or a paired association, but it's not going to correspond to the image of a sexy mate or the constituents of a prepositional phrase. I believe in the fairly standard view that cognitive abilities consist of some sequence or network of more elementary information processes, and that the elementary information processes are the kinds of things that neurons and simple neural nets can do—that is the level where a cognitive scientist might hand the baton to the physiologist and go fishing. But most important, this hierarchical explanation is needed whether an ability is learned or innate, just as the same sequence of instructions can either be programmed into a computer's memory by the user or burned into a ROM at the factory (a crude analogy, I know).

MG: In your book you constantly argue from concrete, almost home-spun everyday examples from ordinary language use to make strong arguments for the genetic basis of language. Could you speak for a moment about the study of linguistics and how it approaches a problem empirically so as to allow the use of those examples?

SP: Actually, both in the book and in my day-to-day research, I try to get data of very different kinds to converge before concluding anything. The most commonly used data in linguistics are judgments about whether some word or sentence sounds natural to a speaker of the language, and what the speaker takes it to mean. It's a kind of psychophysics done on oneself and one's readers, a lot like a demonstration that a Necker cube flips or that isoluminant pictures lack depth. Sometimes, to get higher-precision data on squishy cases I get numerical ratings of grammaticality or meaning from sophomores, but it's the same kind of data, and the judgments and ratings always coincide. (In fact, the F-ratios are often in the 600s, so these studies can get published in the psychology journals where they would otherwise reject anything that seemed too "linguistic.") Generally the linguistic judgments are the most information-rich data, but it's also important to bolster any conclusion by other means. That is because some pattern in a person's judgments may not have been caused by a rule of grammar implemented in his brain but by some set of individual cases that fossilized in the language centuries ago and have been memorized individually.

Take the claim I am currently working on, that regular past tense and plural forms are usually assembled on-line by a mental rule, but irregular ones are retrieved or analogized from memory. You begin with the simple observation that new verbs entering the language automatically get regular forms—*fax, faxed, faxing, faxes.* This suggests some rule that adds *-ed* or *-s,* but that is just a beginning, the level of detail that connectionist memory models can also handle.

From linguistics, you can add a couple of more subtle phenomena. Verbs based on noun roots can't have past tenses listed with their roots in memory (nouns inherently don't have past tenses), and they turn out to be always regular, even when their sound pattern would seem to call out for an irregular form—hence *flied out* and *ringed the city,* not *flew out* and *rang the city.* This confirms that the process creating regular forms is a default operation that applies whenever memory doesn't supply a form. Second, people accept *mice-infested* and *men-bashing* but not *rats-infested* and *guys-bashing.* Say the compounding operation takes two words from memory and glues them together. *Mice* and *men* are in memory, because they are unpredictable, whereas *rats* and *guys* are not, because they can be generated by rule when needed. Therefore the compounding operation finds *mice* in lexical memory and can glue it to *infested,* but can't find *rats* and has to use *rat.*

Now go to the laboratory, and you can show that both these effects can be replicated in ratings by sophomores, and in experiments where you elicit new words from preschool children. Also, sophomores give low ratings and slow reaction times to low-frequency irregular forms such as *strive— strove* and unfamiliar-sounding ones such as *nist—nust* (because of their weak memory traces) but give high ratings and quick reaction times to low-frequency regular forms such as *stint—stinted* and unfamiliar-sounding ones such as *ploamph—ploamphed* (because they don't have to be retrieved from memory, so the weakness of any memory trace is irrelevant). Now look at naturalistic speech errors in children: kids overapply the regular rule, saying things such as *buyed,* and the errors are not correlated either in time or over words with how many forms such as *tied* or *fried* their parents use, suggesting that the errors are rule products, not analogies from memory.

Finally, go to the neuropsychology clinic. A postdoc in my lab, Michael Ullman, has shown that patients with memory disorders and unimpaired grammar, such as Alzheimer's, are fine with regular verbs and with nonsense verbs such as *wugged* but often make errors on irregulars, such as *swimmed*. Patients with impaired grammar but less impaired memory retrieval, such as Broca's aphasics, have trouble with regular verbs and nonsense verbs, but less trouble with irregulars. The data of the linguist from everyday speech and the other kinds of data, at least in this case, fit together almost perfectly.

More generally, Chomsky's argument for the innateness of the language system is based on the discovery that there is information in people's judgments of words and sentences that is not in the input they heard as children. To make the claim more precise and concrete, the psychologist Peter Gordon ran an experiment showing that preschoolers say *mice-eater* but never *rats-eater,* even though one can estimate that they have never heard their parents use either kind of construction and thus could not have learned the distinction from the input; it must have come from the way their lexicons are inherently organized vis-à-vis their grammars. And there are other kinds of data that line up with the claim from linguistic examples: children's precocity at mastering fine points of grammar, even the useless ones; various syndromes in which severely retarded people have intact language; language universals that cannot be attributed to mere utility; the uniform grammatical sophistication across cultures and subcultures despite vast differences in other measures of cultural sophistication; and, perhaps most interesting, cases where children create a grammatically more sophisticated language than the one they hear from their parents.

MG: And needless to say, I assume these kind of analyses work for all languages. They are not flukes of English.

SP: Most immediately, we find the family of phenomena related to regular and irregular morphology in other languages, such as French and Arabic. The best comparison is German, because its statistics are completely different from English. Its version of the plural *-s* and participle *-ed* applies to a *minority* of words, not a majority; the majority of words are irregular. But the suffixes show almost the entire set of effects we find in the English versions, quirks and all—the frequency and similarity effects, the *mice-infested/rats-infested* effect, the *flied out* effect, about a dozen in all. This shows that the hallmarks of a mental rule are not an epiphenomenon of the supposedly "rule-governed" inflection being the majority of cases in the child's experience. They involve a qualitative difference in the way that the brain computes a rule and the way it looks up items in memory.

There's no doubt that languages differ a lot. But I think the evidence is that the same kinds of computational machinery are used in all of them—the division into components, the kinds of data structures used in each component such as nouns and verbs and lexical and phrasal heads, and so on. Different languages use each of these gadgets to different extents, giving the appearance of radical differences. For example, in many native American languages you can build an entire sentence out of a verb by sticking strings of prefixes and suffixes onto it that specify key properties of the verb's arguments, without having to select and place a bunch of noun phrases. It seems completely different from English. But then we have this silly little agreement rule—*the girl eats* versus *the girls eat*—that is essentially the same mechanism. "The" isn't doing much in English; if it disappeared, no one would miss it. It's computationally costly to use and even harder to learn, but English children use it correctly more than 90 percent of the time by the time they turn four. This suggests that the mental algorithms necessary for supposedly radically different languages are available to all humans.

MG: Well, if language is to be understood in this biological sense, in how our species actually operates as opposed to how nineteenth-century grammarians would like us to speak and write, do you see the language cultists such as William Safire as Johnny-come-lately technologists? I mean all of us like sex in the biological sense, but some of us are artists.

SP: Yes, quite right. The guidelines for good style, standardized "proper" grammar, and so on, are at their best technological add-ons that help us use language for purposes that it was not designed for, basically, putting esoteric thoughts on paper for the benefit of strangers. It's an important technology but it is quite different (and far less interesting) than the basic unconscious grammar that we all use to put words together in ordinary conversation. An analogy might be the rules for an illegal defense in basketball compared to the motor control programs for bipedal locomotion. And at its worst, "proper" grammar is just plain dumb, like the screwball rules against *hopefully*, split infinitives, *Everybody returned to their seats*, and so on.

Actually, the so-called "language mavens" such as Safire are more like witch doctors than technologists. Like many linguists, I am always astounded at how ignorant they are about language. It's not just that they don't know this week's version of formal Chomskyan theory; they can't work through freshman problems of grammatical analysis (such as telling a verb from an adjective), and they have no knowledge of the basic facts of English—what kinds of idioms and constructions there are, and how they are used and pronounced. It comes from a general condescension about the speech of the common person, which they consistently underestimate, and ultimately from a nonscientific, uncurious attitude—like many people, they are blasé about unconscious mental processes that work most of the time.

MG: Do you see language as a system separate and distinct from those brain processes that allow for complex thought?

SP: To a large extent, yes. For one thing, the algorithms for grammar cut across the logic of conceptual categories, as in the *mice-eaters* who eat mice differing from the *rat-eaters* who eat rats. Grammar is a communications protocol, not our knowledge database or our inference system. Moreover it is a protocol that has to interface the ear, the mouth, and the mind. So it's no surprise that it doesn't reflect any one of them directly, but has a logic of its own. Also, you find language and general intelligence dissociating in many populations—beginning with toddlers, who are grammatical geniuses but incompetent at just about everything else. In Williams Syndrome, hydrocephalus, and Alzheimer's Disease, you can find intact grammar despite severe deficits in general intelligence, and in some cases of aphasia and genetically transmitted language impairment you find the opposite.

Of course they cannot be completely separate. Language has to interface with the conceptual world, so there has to be a level of semantic representation that is built out of the same kinds of primitives as concepts. When we use language we are engaging in a kind of interpersonal interaction that must involve social reasoning processes. And at the lower neural levels I surely wouldn't expect language to use green neurons and complex thought to use red neurons or anything like that.

MG: Many scientists are now trying to understand the neural basis of language. There are many new imaging techniques (PET, functional MRI, ERPs) and laboratories all over the world are studying language processes and looking for patterns of cerebral activation. What is your opinion of this work? Are they asking the right question? Or is perhaps the answer to how the brain enables language to be found more in considering the properties of local circuits?

SP: Ultimately the answer is in the local circuitry that actually does the computing. Methods such as aphasiology and neuroimaging are a bit like using bomb craters and blurred satellite photos to understand the long-distance telephone network. But of course the neural basis of language has to be studied at many scales, and the neuroimaging methods are very exciting and important. The work to date is very intriguing and a good start, but when you look closely at the whole literature you see some problems. David Poeppel, a graduate student in our program, reviewed the three published studies that claimed to have found the areas involved in phonological processing. He found that the overlap in the three teams' lists of "phonology areas" was zero! Poeppel found the same thing in his review of studies that claimed to have found the areas involved in semantic processing—three completely nonoverlapping lists of "semantic areas." Even more depressing, for both the semantics and the phonology areas, is that all of the teams managed to cite studies in the aphasiology literature that they claimed were consistent with their PET finding. Obviously there are some bugs to be worked out.

One of the problems is that none of the teams studying "language processing" has included a linguist or psycholinguist. Their models of language processing just seem to be made up on the spur of the moment. So they'll have some task such as judging whether two syllables end in the same consonant as an example of "phonological processing." Now, any circuitry for phonology is going to be doing much finer-grained analyses than called for in that task—we did not evolve a brain area to press buttons indicating whether a nonsense syllable ends in a consonant. The task surely involves a whole slew of linguistic and cognitive processes other than phonology, such as parsing and remembering words, perhaps orthographic recoding, and the overhead of remembering the task and generating the appropriate button-press. So it's not surprising that the areas that light up after you subtract passive listening are not at all specific to phonology, and could show no overlap with the areas involved in the "phonology" task in some other lab, which might string together some other arbitrary collection of procedures. Likewise in looking for semantic areas, a task such as generating a verb that goes with a noun just doesn't correspond to any cohesive cognitive process, let alone being a test of language.

More generally, I wonder whether PET research so far has taken the methods of experimental psychology too seriously. In standard psychology we need to have the subject do some task with an externalizable yes-or-no answer so that we have some reaction times and error rates to analyze—those are our only data. But with neuroimaging you're looking at the brain directly so you literally don't need the button-press or the overt blurting. I wonder whether we can be more clever in figuring out how to get subjects to think certain kinds of thoughts silently, without forcing them to do some arbitrary classification task as well. I suspect that when you have people do some artificial task and look at their brains, the strongest activity you'll see is in the parts of the brain that are responsible for doing artificial tasks. Still, it's an intriguing beginning and like most cognitive scientists I'm following it eagerly.

MG: Well, it is an exciting story and a superb and fascinating book. I would like to conclude by asking your thoughts about how your studies of language offer insights into mind design.

SP: If language, the quintessential higher cognitive process, is an instinct, maybe the rest of cognition is a bunch of instincts too—complex circuits designed by natural selection, each dedicated to solving a particular family of computational problems posed by the ways of life we adopted millions of years ago. Aside from language, these might include systems for intuitive physics, biology, and psychology, mental maps, habitat, kinship, mating, danger, food, disease, justice, friendship, and self-monitoring. This is very different from the standard conception of some nondescript but all-powerful "culture" from the social sciences, "information processing" from cognitive psychology, or "association cortex" from neuroscience, concepts that I suspect will go the way of "protoplasm" in biology. But admittedly this is a big leap from irregular German participles.

MG: Thank you.

8

Brain and Language
Alfonso Caramazza

Alfonso Caramazza is a professor of psychology at Harvard University. He received a B.A. in psychology from McGill University in 1970 and a Ph.D. from Johns Hopkins University in 1974. He joined the Hopkins faculty in 1974 and taught there first in the Psychology Department and then in the Cognitive Science Department, which he helped create. He taught at Dartmouth College from 1993 to 1995. Although his research has focused on the neuropsychology of language processes, he has also made contributions in the areas of normal psycholinguistics, naive physics, and, more recently, to the study of mechanisms of visual neglect. Caramazza has been the recipient of a Javits Neuroscience Award and an honorary doctorate from the Catholic University of Louvain.

MG: You have studied how brain lesions disrupt language function. How would you contrast current understanding of brain and language function with those that enticed you into the subject twenty years ago?

AC: The most important differences concern our understanding of the structure of language processes and the implications that follow from this understanding for theories of the representation of language in the brain.

Twenty years ago the study of language disorders in brain-damaged patients was dominated by a rather simplistic conception of language processing and a correspondingly simple view of the representation of these processes in the brain. In other words, language was seen as a collection of "skills," the main ones being comprehension, production, reading, writing, repetition, and naming. Each of these skills (except for repetition) was associated with a specific brain region. For example, Wernicke's and Broca's areas were thought to be the centers for language comprehension and production, respectively. This model of language and its representation in the brain was originally proposed by Wernicke and developed by Lichtheim and others at the end of the nineteenth century. The limitations of this model for explaining the different forms of language dysfunction that followed from brain damage soon became apparent and the model lost the dominant status it had had in the "golden age" of behavioral neurology. However, in the 1960s Norman Geshwind managed to reinstate the Wernicke/Lichtheim model as the dominant view of language processing in the brain. Researchers again focused their efforts on the task of describing language disorders in terms of a small set of syndrome types that was expected to result from focal damage to each of the postulated language centers or their connections. We were all concerned with the task of describing the nature of Broca's aphasia, Wernicke's aphasia, conduction aphasia, deep dyslexia, and other such syndromes. The journals were full of papers describing yet another difference between Wernicke's and Broca's aphasics, or between anomic and conduction aphasics, and so on and so forth.

Things are considerably different today. Although the "classical" view still has its adherents—perhaps the majority of researchers in the field—this approach has long since stopped generating interesting results and ideas. Almost all new phenomena and theories have grown out of a new approach to the analysis of language disorders that has come to be known as "cognitive neuropsychology." This approach reflects the coming together of several important developments in the cognitive and neural sciences. Crucial among these is the idea that language ability is the result of the activity of many processing mechanisms operating over many different forms of knowledge. On this view, an understanding of language disorders cannot proceed independently of the explicit articulation of the structure and form of the cognitive representations that are computed in the course of carrying out a linguistic task. Thus, for example, even the simple task of reading aloud a word is thought to implicate a number of distinct types of representations (visual, graphemic, lexical-orthographic, semantic, lexical-phonological, phonological, articulatory) and associated processing mechanisms. Damage to any component of the processing system will result in impairments that will be reflected in any task that implicates that component of processing. Continuing with our example of reading, since lexical-phonological representations are implicated in all speech production tasks, damage that selectively affects these representations will impair not only reading but all speech production tasks (e.g., naming). In this framework, notions like "reading center" are meaningless, since reading is assumed to be the product of a vast network of perceptual/cognitive/motor mechanisms involving many areas of the left and right hemisphere. There is no single brain center for reading, writing, or comprehension. There are only networks of highly specific mechanisms dedicated to the individual operations that comprise a complex task.

Also less than useful are the classical syndrome types (e.g., Broca's aphasia) and the associated syndrome-based research paradigm. The focus is now on the formulation of detailed theories of normal language processing and the way in which the postulated processing mechanisms might be represented in the brain. We are no longer constrained to interpret disorders in terms of a restricted set of syndromes. There can be as many different disorders as there are forms of damage to the complex processing system that underlies language ability. An especially welcome consequence of this approach has been the discovery of many new, theoretically important patterns of language dysfunction.

MG: Before getting to those new patterns, are you saying the study of brain and language has been held back by neurologists applying simplistic ideas about the nature of language to the aphasic patient?

AC: No, I would not single out neurologists for that dubious honor. To the contrary, some of the most sophisticated analyses of language dissolution in brain-damaged subjects were produced by neurologists. The work of Goldstein and Luria are good examples of very detailed, sophisticated analyses of language disorders. And, yes, I am saying that the study of brain and language has been (and is being) held back by simplistic ideas about language and cognition.

Lest I be misunderstood, let me stress that I am not saying that the classical, syndrome-inspired research produced no useful insights into the nature of language processes and the neural mechanisms that subserve them. To the contrary, this work was immensely useful in demonstrating the usefulness of clinical observations as the basis for charting the functional organization of the human brain. However, the approach is very limited both theoretically and methodologically and has long since outlived its usefulness. Perhaps we can come back to this issue later.

MG: Have the new imaging techniques such as PET and functional MRI helped illuminate the problem of how the brain enables language?

AC: The short answer is no. Up to now the results with PET and functional MRI have not appreciably advanced our understanding of the neural mechanisms that underlie language ability beyond what we already knew through other approaches to the study of the functional organization of the human brain. And I am not sure how useful these specific techniques will turn out to be in the longer term. Of course, we are all hoping that with new advances in technology we will be able to get better spatial and temporal resolutions with these techniques. And technological advances will surely introduce more sophisticated, new techniques for the on-line mapping of the brain (magnetoencephalography seems very promising in this regard). This is an exciting period for researchers interested in the functional organization of the human brain. However, it will take more than technological developments in imaging techniques for us to make significant progress in understanding the neural bases for language. We will have to have a much better understanding of the linguistic and cognitive mechanisms that characterize language production and comprehension. That is, we will need highly detailed processing theories of language that will provide the functional pieces that map onto neural events.

MG: Do you think that language will ever be understood at the level of local neural circuitry?

AC: Why not? I cannot imagine how, but then, who would have anticipated one hundred years ago the achievements of molecular biology?

MG: OK, what are the new patterns to be looked for? And is there evidence these new patterns are verified by neuropsychological evidence?

AC: Many new patterns of deficits have been described. Take as an example an observation originally made by my friend Edgar Zurif and myself nearly twenty years ago. We found that patients who were clinically classified as Broca's aphasics showed a pattern of sentence comprehension deficit that has come to be called "asyntactic comprehension"—the failure to understand sentences whose meaning cannot be correctly obtained from the meaning of the words alone, but that require accurate processing of the syntactic structure of the sentence (e.g., compare "the car is being watched by the boy" versus "the girl is being watched by the boy"). This observation was considered to be important in part because it violated expectations based on the Wernicke/Lichtheim model of language representation in the brain, which claimed that Broca's aphasics should have normal comprehension (lesions in the posterior region of the left frontal lobe—Broca's area—should result in language production and not language comprehension deficits). More interesting, because the observed comprehension failure seemed to concern only so-called reversible sentences, it encouraged the conjecture that a common, modality-independent deficit in syntactic processing was responsible for these patients' agrammatic speech production and asyntactic comprehension. This view implied that syntactic processing is subserved by an autonomous neural mechanism that could be damaged selectively. And it encouraged a shift away from the task- or function-based (e.g., repetition, naming, and reading) approach to the classification of disorders and toward a mechanism-based (e.g., syntactic process, working memory, and lexical access) conception of cognitive disorders.

Once we started thinking in terms of cognitive mechanisms, many new patterns of deficits were observed and studied in detail. Continuing with our present example, it was soon discovered that comprehension failure can dissociate from judgments of grammaticality; it was discovered that asyntactic comprehension is found in various types of patients who are not agrammatic, and that not all agrammatic patients show asyntactic comprehension; it was found that the ability to process thematic roles (who does what to whom) can dissociate from the ability to process morphological information; it was found that there are forms of agrammatic production that are found only in one modality of output and not the other (e.g., agrammatic writing but not speaking), and so on and so forth. The various patterns of association and dissociation of sentence comprehension and production deficits show that brain damage can selectively affect different components of the complex machinery of sentence processing.

What is important to emphasize here is not just the volume of new results (although that too is important), but the fact that the new results are being found because our approach to the analysis of neurological disorders encourages us to look for them. That is, once we started taking seriously the possibility that we could use the performance of brain-damaged subjects as a window into the structure and organization of normal cognitive processes, we could then use models of normal cognition to guide our expectations about the possible forms of deficits that should be observed following selective damage to part or parts of a cognitive system. And since even a relatively simple task (e.g., writing single words to dictation) implicates many processing components (i.e., auditory, phonological, lexical, orthographic, and motor mechanisms), damage to any part of the network of mechanisms that subserve a task is expected to result in highly specific forms of impairment, each reflecting the structure and role of the particular mechanism affected by damage. In this way we expect to find many more theoretically meaningful patterns of deficits than have been enshrined in the classical syndrome typologies. When seen from this perspective, it becomes clear that clinical syndromes such as Broca's aphasia, deep dyslexia, and visual neglect represent no more than theoretically arbitrary groupings of symptoms, not to be privileged over other patterns of deficits that may prove to be of greater theoretical value. And there are many such patterns. I've already alluded to the case of deficits of sentence processing where it has been clearly demonstrated that there are many different forms of sentence comprehension and production impairment that do not fit into any of the classical syndrome types. This variety in the patterns of sentence-processing deficits presumably reflects the fact that brain damage can differentially affect the various components of the complex process of sentence processing. The same principle holds for other perceptual, motor, and cognitive functions. Thus, there have been many reports of theoretically interesting patterns of associations and dissociations of symptoms in the areas of reading, writing, object recognition, spatial processing, memory, and motor planning. I'd be happy to discuss an example from the work of my colleagues and myself if you wish.

In short, in answer to the first part of your question, the important issue is not so much which pattern of deficit to be on the lookout for—there are many in all areas of cognitive neuropsychology—but "how do we use these observations to constrain theories of normal cognitive processing and their representation in the brain?" It is also important to consider how the new analyses of cognitive deficits may help inform therapeutic practice.

As to the second part of your question, I guess I don't understand what you mean by "verified by neuropsychological evidence?" The research we have been talking about *is* neuropsychological research.

MG: Throw a wrench into the brain and exotic patterns of behavior result. Some of them are described, the ones that make sense with ongoing models of linguistic function. But start the other way around. From the study of natural language, can predictions be made about how the representations must look, which is to say be distributed? And do brain-damaged patients verify those predictions?

AC: Good question! But let me deal first with some aspects of the way in which you formulate the premise for your question. In your question you raise the possibility that in neuropsychology there might be a bias in reporting or describing only those patterns of impaired performance that fit our current theoretical positions. You are right to point out that there may be such a bias. But if you are insinuating that the bias problem is more acute in neuropsychology than in other empirical enterprises then I must disagree, or at least challenge you to motivate such a claim. In fact, one could argue that neuropsychology is afflicted by the opposite problem: Because cognitive neuropsychology is strongly rooted in the clinical tradition, which greatly valued the description of new clinical patterns, much of the work is merely descriptive and uninfluenced by a strong theoretical framework. If anything, then, neuropsychology is probably less prone than other branches of the cognitive and neural sciences to "ignore" results that do not fit the dominant theoretical positions.

I also want to briefly take issue with your use of the term "exotic" to describe the patterns of impairment that may be observed in brain-damaged patients. I take issue with the use of this term because it plays into the hands of those psychologists (for example Kosslyn) who are inclined to believe that the performance of brain-damaged patients is somehow alien, bizarre, and marginal to the enterprise of understanding normal cognition and its neural basis. To be sure, the performance of some brain-damaged subjects can be quite startling. For example, there are patients who produce semantic errors in naming a picture (e.g., tiger——>leopard) while concurrently writing the correct response; or patients who when asked to copy a scene correctly reproduce only either the left or right half (depending on whether they have sustained damage to the left or right hemisphere, respectively) of each object in a scene, and so on. So the performance of brain-damaged patients can be "exotic" in the sense of being radically unlike that of normal subjects. But this aspect of patients' performance does not make it necessarily less valuable for constraining theories of normal cognition. On the contrary, it could be argued that it is precisely the "exotic" nature of the performance that gives it special theoretical value, for it may reveal aspects of the system that are ordinarily invisible in the normally functioning system. Brain damage unpacks the closely integrated normal system to reveal its internal structure. And now let me turn to your question: Can we make verifiable predictions from the study of natural language about the types of language impairment that should be observed in brain-damaged patients? There is no simple answer to this question. It all depends on the kind of theory of language one is proposing. Theories of the normal language-processing system do not necessarily have anything to say about how the system can break down under conditions of brain damage. To make predictions about the consequences of brain damage for language performance we need more than a theory of normal language processing: we also need to make appropriate assumptions about the way in which language processes are distributed in the brain and the way in which damage can affect these processes. Thus, for example, if we were to assume (1) that the phonological and orthographic forms of lexical knowledge are independent one from the other, (2) that the two forms of knowledge are subserved by independent neural systems, and (3) that these systems can be damaged selectively, then we would be able to predict a dissociation of these two forms of lexical knowledge in specific cases of brain damage. Similarly, on the assumption that lexical knowledge and syntactic processes are subserved by independent neural systems that can be damaged selectively, we would predict a dissociation between syntactic and lexical processes. Of course, we could also make predictions for many finer-grained dissociations so long as we are willing to assume that highly specific forms of knowledge (e.g., nouns versus verbs) might be represented by independent neural systems. [Parenthetically, I should note that the reverse is not necessarily true: the dissociation between two types of stimuli (e.g., short versus long words) does not require that we assume the existence of corresponding independent representations in a cognitive system (see Caramazza, Hillis, Rapp, and Romani, 1990, *Cognitive Neuropsychology,* for discussion of this issue in the context of claims about the organization of the lexical semantic system).] And as I've already noted, over the past twenty or so years a fairly large number of theoretically interesting dissociations have been reported. These range from dissociations that show the independence of syntactic and lexical-semantic processes, to finer-grained dissociations that show that inflectional and derivational morphological processes are independent one from the other, to dissociations that show that nouns and verbs are represented by independent neural mechanisms. Each of these dissociations falls out naturally from models of normal language processing.

Although I don't want to muddy the waters too much I would like to take a couple of minutes to address the issue of "prediction" in neuropsychological research as you have raised it here. The view of science as the simple testing of predictions derived from theories does not adequately capture the reality of cognitive neuropsychological research. Unfortunately, inferences about normal cognitive processes from the study of the performance of brain-damaged patients are complicated by the fact that these cases constitute experiments of nature over which the experimenter has little control. Unlike the case of laboratory experiments, nature does not strategically place brain lesions so as to accommodate the theoretical interests of neuropsychologists. Thus, for example, patients with brain damage of vascular etiology will have lesions reflecting the vagaries of vascular pathology and not any intrinsic functional organization of the brain. Consequently, any one patient will present a complex pattern of dysfunction of unknown form; so that even when we have very good information about lesion site we still don't know which cognitive mechanism(s) has been affected by the damage. And since to test claims about the structure of cognitive processes we must know what experiment nature has carried out for us—that is, we must know which cognitive mechanism(s) has been affected by the brain damage—our first order of business is to do just that. But note that we are being forced to use the performance of the patient both to establish which cognitive mechanism(s) has been affected by brain damage and to test claims about the structure of that (or of a related) mechanism. This dual use of the performance of brain-damaged subjects has important methodological implications for the use of impaired performance to infer the structure of normal cognitive processes. This is not the place to discuss in detail these matters, but allow me to simply state the most controversial implication: only single-patient analyses allow valid inferences about normal cognitive processes. This means that the neuropsychological research that is based on patient-group analyses (probably the vast majority) is simply not relevant to the enterprise of determining the structure of cognitive mechanisms and their neural bases. (Historically this is obviously true: virtually all significant insights about cognitive mechanisms and their neural bases have come to us from single-patient analyses.)

Here, however, I want to focus on a more subtle implication that follows from the fact that individual brain-damaged patients constitute (potentially) distinct experiments of nature. Because the exact experimental conditions introduced by nature in each of its experiments are not known a priori but must be inferred from the performance of each patient, the role of prediction in neuropsychological investigations is extremely limited—prediction would be a rather empty exercise without adequate knowledge of the relevant experimental conditions in each experiment. The more useful notion is that of retrodiction (as formulated by Charles Pierce, I think)—in the present context this would refer to the process of working back from patterns of impaired performance to infer the functional locus of damage to a specific cognitive system. The way in which impaired performance is used to constrain theories of normal cognitive processing is as follows: If it is possible to postulate (retrodict) a specific transformation (functional lesion) to a component of a model of normal cognitive processing such that the modified cognitive system can account for the observed patterns of impairment, we can then take the observed performance as support for that model of cognitive processing (over alternative accounts that do not allow retrodiction to plausible functional lesions in those models).

If I am right about the logic of inferences in research with clinical populations, this greatly complicates the inferential process in this area of research and helps define an appropriate "methodology." On this view, we cannot simply get a patient (or group of patients) of one type or another, make a "prediction," and carry out the next parametric manipulation hoping to meaningfully contribute to the joint enterprise of understanding normal cognition and its neural basis. This theoretically passive role will not do—it can lead only to uninterpretable results. When a brain-damaged subject walks in our testing room we do not know the aspect of the cognitive system for which his or her performance will be relevant. To be sure, an initial clinical evaluation will narrow the range of possibilities, but not to a theoretically useful level—clinical evaluations (e.g., deep dyslexia, agrammatism) consider only gross behavioral features that do not adequately reveal the precise nature of the relevant deficit in any one patient. Before we can even begin to think of possible "predictions," we must establish the possible locus (or loci) of functional damage to the cognitive system of the case under investigation. The useful investigation requires that we engage in a complex process of retrodiction and prediction: on the basis of initial observations we make a first-pass hypothesis about a possible locus of functional impairment (retrodiction); on the basis of this hypothesis about functional damage to a specific cognitive system we generate predictions about possible outcomes on various tasks; we evaluate the actual outcomes to confirm the correctness of the hypothesized functional impairment and make appropriate adjustments (retrodiction); and then on to the next iteration until we have reached an adequate level of confidence about the hypothesized transformation to the cognitive system. This research strategy quickly converges on results that strongly constrain theoretical claims.

I'm sorry to make things this complicated but, unfortunately, that's the way things are, and it doesn't help to pretend otherwise.

MG: Let's talk about the lexicon and polysemous words. There are 26 meanings to the word "line." Are there brain-damaged patients that lose specific capacities, lose the ability to use some meanings of the word but not others? If so, what does that tell us about the organization of the brain's lexicon?

AC: To my knowledge no one has reported cases of selective deficit of specific meanings of polysemous words. Of course, this could simply reflect the fact that no one has carefully looked for such deficits. But there are reports of highly selective deficits of word meaning that affect only some conceptual categories and not others. The best known cases are the category-specific deficits for animate versus inanimate objects first clearly analyzed by Elizabeth Warrington in the 1970s. Since those early reports, there have been many others that have clearly established that damage to the semantic system need not be all-or-none but can selectively affect some categories while leaving others relatively unaffected. A clear implication of these deficits is that categorical information plays a crucial role in the organization of the semantic system. However, the way in which categorical information is represented remains controversial. Thus, for example, War-

rington and her collaborators argued that categorical structure emerges from the differential roles that visual and
functional information play in the definition of living and
nonliving things—presumably visual properties are more
important in defining the meaning of living things than nonliving things. My colleagues and I have argued, instead, that
categorical structure emerges from the differential roles that
diverse semantic features, independently of their sensory/
nonsensory status, play in the definition of various categories. On this view, the visual/functional distinction of specific
properties of objects is given no more weight than any other
distinction between properties. Thus, although in both cases
category structure emerges as a consequence of the types of
properties that define objects in different categories, only on
one account is a sensory/nonsensory distinction relevant
(Warrington's).

Perhaps even more striking are the reports of selective
deficits of one member of homonym pairs. Some years ago,
Gabriele Miceli and I found that patients with frontal lobe
lesions were likely to have difficulties in producing verbs
whereas patients with temporal lobe lesions were more likely
to have problems in producing nouns. More recently, Argye
Hillis and I reported several patients who are impaired in
processing the verb form of words such as *watch, crack,* and
dress, but not their noun form, and patients who show the
opposite form of deficit—impaired in processing the noun
form of the homonym pair and not the verb form. Even
more striking is the fact that these category-specific deficits
for grammatical class can be modality-specific as well. That
is, the selective deficit for words of a specific grammatical
class (e.g., nouns or verbs) can be found to occur only in
writing or only in speaking. We have now reported four patients who show such dissociations, including a patient who

shows difficulties in processing verbs but not nouns in one modality (either oral or written production) and the opposite pattern of difficulties in the other modality. These patterns of dissociations suggest (1) that phonological and orthographic forms of lexical knowledge are independent of each other, (2) that grammatical class information is represented independently and redundantly in the phonological and the orthographic lexicons, and (3) that these lexicons are organized by grammatical class. These are rather strong claims about the nature of lexical organization that we would not have reached from current psycholinguistic or linguistic research. And, in fact, our results do not sit comfortably with those connectionists who would dispense with abstract information such as grammatical class nor with those psycholinguists who dislike the idea that grammatical information is represented at the level of lexical forms.

MG: To say that phonological and orthographic forms are dissociated does not mean that they are independent. If they were independent they would be unrelated, so that the spoken form /*dawg*/ and the written form *dog* could mean totally different things. There is some dependence between them; it is commonly accepted that children learn the phonological forms first and only later learn to associate orthographic forms with those spoken words; learning to read and write is not "independent" of prelearned speech. If what you mean by independent is that you can speak without being literate and vice versa, that is hardly a startling claim. Could you define more carefully what you mean by independent in this case?

AC: By independent I mean that the two forms of knowledge are functionally and neurally autonomous. In the context of the present discussion this means that in reading and in writing, lexical orthographic forms are directly related to meaning without the mediation of phonology. Thus, it is assumed that in reading, the graphemic representation computed from the visual stimulus serves to activate a lexical orthographic representation, which, in turn, activates its corresponding lexical semantic representation. Similarly, in writing, a semantic representation activates a lexical orthographic representation, which then serves as the basis for subsequent letter-processing stages. As you well know, this view of the organization of lexical knowledge is not without its critics. However, the data from neuropsychology would seem to leave little room for discussion of this matter: as I pointed out earlier, there is unequivocal evidence for the selective sparing of lexical orthographic forms in the face of severe deficits in processing lexical phonological forms; the reverse pattern of dissociation has also been reported.

Perhaps I can make clearer what I mean by the term "independent" through a different example. A few years ago, Gabriele Miceli and I analyzed in some detail the spelling performance of an Italian dysgraphic patient. Among other interesting features of this patient's performance was the fact that he made many transposition errors such as *carote* (carrots)——→*racote* or *catore* or *corate*, etc. He also made a nonnegligible number of transposition errors in spelling words with geminate or double letters (e.g., *cavallo* [horse]). The errors involving the double letters always took the following form: *cavallo*——→*cavvalo* or *calavvo;* he never made errors such as *cavallo*——→*calavlo* or *calalvo.* That is, transposition errors involving double letters always concerned both letters of the pair. Along with other observations, this result led us to conclude that graphemic structures represent information about the identity of graphemes *independently* of the information about their number. This means that geminate clusters are not represented by two graphemes but by one grapheme with the specification that it is to be doubled. This representational claim allows us to explain how it is possible to independently move the information about doubling to a different place in the word (*cavallo* ———→*cavvalo*) or to independently move information about grapheme identity while leaving behind information about doubling (*cavallo*———→ *calavvo*) of the letter. (I should point out that the representational claims about geminates are a natural part of the more general claim that graphemic representations have a multidimensional structure in which different dimensions represent different types of information: grapheme identity, consonant/vowel status, gemination, and graphosyllabic structure.)

I chose this example in part to show how cognitive neuropsychological research can lead to highly detailed claims about the structure of language and cognitive processes. That is, I want to stress that there is a two-way street between cognitive theory and neuropsychological research: cognitive theory guides the investigation of cognitive deficits and, in turn, the analysis of impaired cognitive performance can be used to inform theories of normal cognitive processing.

MG: Is your argument that the cost of organizing the mental lexicon syntactically (the fact that words like *light* have to be stored separately as a noun and as a verb and as an adjective, for example) is more than compensated for by the advantage that inflections (which are different in different syntactic categories) can be stored apart from the words they inflect? In other words, the economy of not having to store *light, lights, lighted, lighting,* and *lit* as separate verbs more than compensates for the cost of storing *light* in several parts of speech.

AC: Actually the argument is slightly different. The trade-off is between processing efficiency and space/organizational constraints. It is true that by specifying grammatical information redundantly in each lexical component—the phonological, the orthographic, and the lexical-semantic components—the system is not very parsimonious. But what we lose in parsimony by having multiple representations we might gain in processing efficiency. If we were to assume that lexical forms are morphologically structured such that stems are represented independently of inflectional affixes, we would have to find some means of constraining which stems go with which affixes. The principal determinant of this pairing is the grammatical class of the stem; for example, verbal affixes are attached to verb stems. Thus, grammatical class information is used at the level of lexical form in guiding morphological composition. My point is simply that since grammatical information is needed at the level of lexical form, it would make engineering sense (read processing efficiency) to represent at this level of processing the grammatical information needed to constrain morphological composition.

Having invoked parsimony, I should note that it is not at all clear to me that it is a relevant consideration at this stage of the game in thinking about the organization of language in the brain. We are still far from having detailed neural theories of language. To those of us who have dedicated a good part of our lives to understanding the structure of language processes and their organization in the brain it is sometimes frustrating that we are still unable to make detailed claims about the representation of language processes in the brain. Thus, taking the case of lexical representation as an example, it is clear that we have been able to generate fairly strong neuropsychological evidence for the compositional structure of the lexical system, but we are still unable to say which brain structures subserve each of the identified cognitive mechanisms. However, there are also many rewards for those of us who work with brain-damaged subjects. For example, being able to make sense of a pattern of language dysfunction in a patient gives us the hope that we will be able to figure out the nature of the deficit and possibly to develop therapeutic techniques that may help recover some of the lost functions. And, of course, we continue to hope that the neuropsychologically motivated theory of language that is being developed through the analysis of aphasic disorders will serve as the basis for a nontrivial theory of the organization of language processes in the brain.

MG: Thank you.

V

Imagery and Consciousness

9

Mental Imagery
Stephen M. Kosslyn

Stephen M. Kosslyn is Professor of Psychology at Harvard University and an Associate Psychologist in the Department of Neurology at the Massachusetts General Hospital. He received his B.A. in 1970 from UCLA and his Ph.D. from Stanford University in 1974, both in psychology, and taught at Johns Hopkins, Harvard, and Brandeis Universities before joining the Harvard faculty as Professor of Psychology in 1983.

His work focuses on the nature of visual mental imagery and high-level vision, as well as applications of psychological principles to visual display design. He has published over 125 papers on these topics, co-edited five books, and authored or co-authored five books. His books include Image and Mind *(1980),* Ghosts in the Mind's Machine *(1983),* Wet Mind: The New Cognitive Neuroscience *(with O. Koenig, 1992),* Elements of Graph Design *(1994), and* Image and Brain: The Resolution of the Image Debate *(1994). Kosslyn has received numerous honors, including the National Academy of Sciences Initiatives in Research Award and the Jean-Louis Signoret Prix.*

MG: You played a major role in establishing the phenomenon of mental imagery as a tractable scientific problem. You started your work in the area of cognitive psychology but now have moved squarely into cognitive neuroscience. Why?

SK: The short answer is that facts about the brain allowed me to answer questions that seemed unanswerable using purely behavioral measures.

MG: And the long answer?

SK: My predecessors developed methods to study the *functions* of imagery, such as its role in memory and reasoning. I was interested in a different set of questions, concerned with the *structure* of the representations that underlie the experience of visual mental imagery. I consider these representations as types of data structures in an information processing system. In my original experiments, starting with one on image scanning in 1973, I used response time to try to infer properties of such representations. For example, I used response time as a kind of "mental tape measure" in the scanning experiments, with the goal of showing that mental image representations embody spatial extent. Introspectively, images seem to have pictorial properties, which seemed to make sense if the representation itself is a kind of spatial pattern. This type of representation would depict, rather than describe, the visual properties of an object or scene. If so, I reasoned, then people should require more time to shift attention farther distances across objects in their mental images (even when their eyes were closed). And this is just what happened: The farther people had to scan across an object to locate a named property, the longer it took.

The same year that the original scanning paper appeared, Pylyshyn published his critique of mental imagery. He argued that mental images are stored as "propositional" representations, no different in kind from the representations that underlie language. In his view, the pictorial properties of imagery that are evident to introspection are entirely epiphenomenal; they play no part in information processing. These properties are like the heat from a light bulb when one reads, which plays no role in the reading process. Thus began the so-called "imagery debate," which has kept me focused on imagery all these years.

The imagery debate was *not* about whether people experience mental images; all parties agreed that they do. It was about the nature of the underlying internal representations. Do the same types of representations underlie the experience of visual mental images and language, or is there something special about at least some of the representations used in imagery? I naively thought that the results from my scanning experiments spoke to this issue; they did, after all, show that a property of imagery that is evident to introspection—spatial extent—affects information processing. But this finding was easily explained in other ways. Some researchers argued that the visual properties of objects are represented as lists, and more time was required to iterate further down these lists; such lists preserve ordinal spatial relations, but do not depict information—they are not images. Some others argued that the instructions for the task led the subjects to use these types of representations (unconsciously) to mimic what they would do in the corresponding perceptual situation. At its heart, the problem was that the theories were too underconstrained. When faced with additional data, people could alter their notions about the properties of processes in order to preserve properties of their favorite representation. I found this state of affairs very frustrating. Presumably, there is a fact to the matter: When one has the experience of imagery, at least one of the underlying representations either has or does not have depictive properties.

So, why cognitive neuroscience? Neuroscientific information provided a way to ground this research, to remove some of the degrees of freedom that made it so easy to explain the behavioral results. When I did "dry mind" research, ignoring the brain, I argued that an image representation is like a pattern of points in an array in a computer. When I learned that multiple topographical mapped areas in the macaque cortex are used in visual perception, this made theorizing much more concrete and direct, and also provided grounds for making strong predictions: If one could show that at least some of these topographical mapped areas are active when one closes one's eyes and forms visual mental images, this would go a large part of the way toward demonstrating that image representations are depictive. And if imagery were disrupted when these areas are damaged, one could not argue that the representations they support are purely epiphenomenal. Moreover, Pylyshyn had raised a number of potential paradoxes; for example, does the "mind's eye" need a "mind's eye's brain"? And does the mind's eye's brain require its own mind's eye to "see" the images? Considering the roles of other areas that are connected to these topographically organized areas provided a handle on these issues. Turning to the brain not only helped me to characterize the questions, but invited additional approaches toward answering them—and these methods produced data that were more difficult to explain in other ways.

MG: Well, before we go into what your journey into brain science has taught you, would you care to define what you think the goals of cognitive neuroscience ought to be or might be? Your first thoughts simply reference some well-known traditional neuroscience work. Is cognitive neuroscience a new intellectual discipline or simply traditional neuropsychology dressed up in a new phrase?

SK: Cognitive neuroscience is a good illustration of how the whole can be more than the sum of its parts. In my view, cognitive neuroscience is an interdisciplinary melding of studies of the brain, of behavior and cognition, and of computational systems that have properties of the brain and that can produce behavior and cognition. I don't think of cognitive neuroscience as the intersection of these areas, as the points of overlap, but rather as their union: It is not just that each approach constrains the others, but rather that each approach provides insights into different aspects of the same phenomena.

When you ask about "traditional neuropsychology," I assume that you don't mean the early work by clinicians that was designed to detect brain injury; this work was extremely empirical, and not aimed at understanding the underlying mechanisms. The more interesting comparison, I think, is to "cognitive neuropsychology." Both cognitive neuropsychology and cognitive neuroscience make use of theory developed in cognitive psychology and cognitive science to characterize the nature of the behavior or cognitive process to be studied. And both enterprises want to specify how information processing occurs; indeed, both sets of researchers often rely on computational models. Moreover, both enterprises exploit tasks and methodologies that have been developed in cognitive psychology and cognitive science (and these tactics and methods are often more sophisticated than those used in traditional neuropsychology). The major contrast between cognitive neuroscience and cognitive neuropsychology is revealed by the different nouns in their names. Cognitive neuroscience is an attempt to understand how cognition arises from brain processes; the focus is on the brain, as the term "neuroscience" implies. We don't want to separate the theory of information processing from the theory of the brain as a physical mechanism. Cognitive neuropsychology, at least as characterized by Caramazza, Shallice, and others, focuses on the functional level per se. They want to understand information processing independently of properties of the wetware itself.

A complete cognitive neuroscience theory would specify more than just the component processes and principles of their interaction. In addition, it would specify how each process is instantiated in the brain, and how brain circuits produce the input/output mappings accomplished by each process. This understanding would extend down to individual types of receptors, channels, and ultimately to the genes. Given these goals, it seems clear that cognitive neuroscience must move closer to neurobiology. But it will not simply become neurobiology: Cognitive neuroscience adds methods and techniques to study, and conceptualize, how the brain gives rise to cognition and behavior.

MG: For some, the componental nature of the new cognitive psychology translated nicely into the neurologic clinic where bizarre dissociations are the rule. Perhaps, it was felt, processing modules could be selectively hit with brain lesions and therein provide support for a cognitive formulation. Yet would you not agree the *objective* of a mature cognitive neuroscience would be to ascertain the algorithms active in translating structural physiological data into psychological function?

SK: Yes, that's part of the objective. We want to understand not just the component processes, but also the details of how neurons actually compute these functions—the algorithms, if you will.

MG: Isn't this what David Marr had in mind? What would you say is Marr's greatest contribution, looked at with the cold lenses of hindsight some dozen years after his death?

SK: I think cognitive neuroscience owes an enormous amount to David Marr. Marr provided the first concrete example of how one could rigorously combine neuroscientific, computational, and psychophysical findings and concepts. He provided an illustration of how the different sorts of information could illuminate a single problem, providing insights into different aspects of it. Even though the details of his particular theory of visual processing may not stand the test of time, his style of thinking and approach are nothing short of brilliant. In my view, one of Marr's best ideas is his conception of a "theory of the computation," which has received surprisingly little attention. He was unhappy with the tendency in Artificial Intelligence research to make up theories purely on the basis of intuition, and wanted theories to be rooted in careful logical analyses and empirical investigation. Marr argued that one should develop a theory of the computation whenever one proposes a particular decomposition into processing components. Such a theory rests on a detailed analysis of what information processing problems must be solved in order for a system to be capable of having certain abilities; the abilities are determined empirically, from studies of normal cognition and behavior and studies of cognition and behavior following brain damage. Once one has a theory of the goal of a processing component or set of components, what they're for, one then is in a position to theorize about the specific representations and algorithms that are used. I can't possibly do justice to these ideas here, so let me simply recommend strongly that people go back and read Marr's book, if only to understand his style of thinking. Too much of his good advice has been neglected by contemporary "connectionist" modelers, who often seem to make up theories at the level of the algorithm as they go along.

MG: Does Marr's approach guide you?

SK: I try to develop "poor man's versions" of theories of what is computed. I simply don't have Marr's gift for seeing how to formalize vaguely specified problems. In my new book, *Image and Brain,* I've tried to use Marr's approach in a qualitative way, and even this seems preferable to relying solely on intuition and attempts to explain empirical results.

MG: OK, let's take the problem of mental imagery and go through how the brain side of the story has evolved over the last ten years. First, what has the lesion work instructed us about imaginal processes?

SK: Two main messages emerge from the lesion work: First, imagery and like-modality perception share many common mechanisms, even though they do not rely on identical mechanisms. One often sees corresponding deficits in imagery and perception (such as unilateral visual neglect, as documented by Bisiach and his colleagues), but also can find patients who have intact imagery and deficient perception (e.g., as documented by Behrmann and her colleagues) and vice versa (e.g., as demonstrated by Charcot, Brain, and others many years ago). The finding that imagery shares many mechanisms with perception is very important because it is much easier to understand perception than to understand imagery: Not only is perception rooted in observable stimulus events (which can be experimentally manipulated and correlated with psychological events), but also we have very good animal models of our perceptual systems and hence have come to understand the underlying neural systems in considerable detail. We can "piggyback" on this understanding when developing theories of imagery.

Second, results from lesion studies have shown that imagery is not a single process. For example, the "what vs. where" that Ungerleider and Mishkin introduced in visual perception also extends to imagery (e.g., as demonstrated by Levine, Calvanio, and Farah). Moreover, different imagery abilities can be selectively disrupted by brain damage. For example, my colleagues and I have described patients who can generate and maintain images (at least of the types we tested), but have difficulty rotating objects in images.

MG: Are you really comfortable with these conclusions? Isn't the lesion method full of difficulties? For example, couldn't the dissociation you mention simply be reflecting task difficulty? Surely it is more difficult to rotate an image and given that, the brain damage itself rears its ugly head?

SK: The lesion method, like all others, has potential problems and has to be used with care. For example, as you note, more difficult tasks will not be performed as well by patients with brain damage—and so a dissociation may say nothing about the existence of distinct processing components. But this is not an insurmountable problem. One way to deal with it is to design tasks that are equated for difficulty. The most straightforward way to do this is to pretest age- and education-matched control subjects, and adjust the materials until these subjects require the same mean time and have the same mean error rates in the tasks. Another response to this sort of possible problem is to obtain a "double dissociation," to find two patients with the opposite pattern of deficits. However, even when one does find a clean double dissociation, such a result is not airtight evidence for the existence of separate processing components; Shallice's book has a nice discussion of the applicability of the logic of double dissociation, and in 1992 Intriligator and I published a paper (in this journal) that touched on this topic.

MG: Aren't there better approaches? For example, can a cognitively impoverished disconnected right hemisphere carry out mental rotation tasks or can only the cognitively superior left hemisphere?

SK: As far as I can tell, all methods have their drawbacks and their strengths. Hemispheric dissociations are a valuable source of converging data, but they too are sometimes ambiguous. For example, there are reports that patients with unilateral left- and unilateral right-hemisphere lesions have deficits in mental rotation, and there are divided-visual-field studies of normal subjects that report that the right hemisphere is better than the left hemisphere, that the left hemisphere is superior, or that both hemispheres are equally effective. I don't find this surprising: Any complex task is likely to be performed by many component processes working in concert, some of which may be more effective in one hemisphere and some of which may be more effective in the other hemisphere—and depending on the precise nature of the task, different components may contribute more or less to the overall processing, leading to hemispheric differences in performance.

MG: So, what are the strengths of the lesion approach?

SK: I find lesion data particularly useful for testing predictions: If one posits that the posterior parietal lobe does function X, patients with damage to this area had better show deficits in tasks that rely on this function. Similarly, if one claims that a particular region is the seat of a specific processing component, then damage to other regions should not affect that function (when factors such as overall activation level and diaschesis are controlled). Lesion work can play a critical role in telling one whether a specific area is necessary or sufficient for a specific type of processing.

In addition, selective deficits following brain damage have enormous heuristic value; even though these deficits do not always reflect the loss of individual processing components in isolation, they sometimes may. And thus they can serve as a useful source of hypotheses; they can inform one's theory of what is computed. Harking back to Marr, his theory of how shapes are stored in long-term memory was influenced by Warrington's finding that some types of brain-damaged patients could not identify objects seen from unusual points of view. There is no guarantee that the hypothesis is correct, of course (and I think Marr was off the mark in this case), but that's not the point: The dissociations following brain damage can lead one to formulate interesting hypotheses, which in turn lead to further empirical investigation.

In general, lesion data, like all other sorts, are best used as one source of converging evidence. There are lots of *potential* problems with any method. This doesn't mean that these potential problems are actual problems in any specific case.

MG: Converging evidence is important, to be sure. However, neuroscience often seems to depend on double dissociation as the solid test of theories about cognitive function. Perhaps convergent evidence is called for only when a double dissociation cannot be found. For example, it would be hard to find a patient that can rotate an image they can't generate!

SK: Actually I would predict that there should be patients who can rotate objects in images but have difficulty generating them; in the typical rotation task, the stimulus remains in view, and the task does not require activating information stored in long-term memory (in Cooper and Shepard's famous tasks, the subjects usually are simply asked whether a visible figure is facing normally or is mirror-reversed, regardless of its angular orientation). In any case, double dissociations are only one of a number of sources of evidence that can converge to support a particular theory of cognitive processing.

MG: Well, this notion of converging data is a version of the meta-analysis approach, is it not? Who was it that said if you see a pile of shit, you know there must be a pony in there somewhere? Psychological processes are full of probabilistic events that allow meta-analysis to work. When it comes to biological processes, however, the approach seems inappropriate. Either you know something or you don't. Either something is built in a certain way or it is not.

SK: I don't think of converging evidence as a version of the meta-analysis approach. That approach is most commonly used to find statistical significance over a set of individual studies, each of which may have reported nonsignificant findings. In the approach I advocate, each individual finding should be statistically significant. That's not at issue. What's at issue is how to *interpret* the individual results. And it is here that convergent evidence is so important, given that results from any given method usually are open to alternative interpretations. To say that "you know something or you don't" is correct if we define "something" as a specific result; one knows that a patient with lesion X, or with information sent only to hemisphere Y, does this-and-that well but not this-and-the-other-thing. The results themselves do not imply that one knows that a specific process exists or that a particular sequence of information processing takes place; it's up to the theorist to interpret the data.

In my view the convergent evidence approach does two things for you. First, it helps you figure out whether a given finding is due to some kind of artifact or methodological problem. There are plenty of such possible snags with any method, but these are *potential* problems and need not necessarily bedevil a given experiment. The best way to know whether to take a specific set of results seriously, in my view, is to see whether it lines up with results from other methods (which also have potential problems, but different ones).

Second, the converging evidence approach does more than simply validate the different methods. It fleshes out the nature of the phenomena to be studied, and provides insights into different aspects of the underlying mechanisms. A good convergent evidence approach uses the results from one type of study to guide other types of studies. For example, results from our recent fMRI studies suggest that only some subjects activate primary visual cortex during imagery, although the other subjects do activate other regions of the occipital lobe. This result leads to an hypothesis about processing: Do subjects who activate primary visual cortex have more vivid images than those who do not activate this region? If so, they should be able to answer questions that require high-resolution images better than subjects who don't activate primary visual cortex, but there should be no difference if low-resolution imagery is all that is necessary. Similarly, this line of thinking leads to asking whether primary visual cortex is necessary for high-resolution images, which could be tested by examining patients who have selective damage to primary visual cortex, but little or no damage to circumstriate regions; will they form fuzzier images than patients with equivalent damage to other parts of the brain? And so forth.

So, different methods are used to ask about different facets of a problem. I think it is important to keep in mind that depending on what particular question you ask, different things count as answers. And depending on the kind of answer you seek, different methods will be more or less appropriate. If you want to know whether a specific area is involved in processing, a brain-scanning study makes sense. If you want to know whether this area is necessary for such processing, a lesion study makes sense, and so forth.

MG: But the convergent evidence approach breaks down if the results don't line up, doesn't it? You mention brain-scanning results. What we have with PET results is, at this point, a set of findings. It now appears impossible to activate, using PET, the frontal eye fields. If PET is tracking activity, how could that be? It now appears the hippocampus is not activated during memory tasks. How could that be? A recent review of language studies finds each investigator has activated different cortical areas for phonological and semantic processing. How could that be?

SK: The convergent evidence approach doesn't imply that the results necessarily must converge . . . only that they will make sense if you do the right experiments and your theory guides you to look for the right characteristics of the data. If you don't design a task properly to engender a specific type of activation, you won't see the brain footprints of that type of processing. And these footprints need not be consistent activation of a single locus. They could be activation of a pattern of areas, of any k of n possible areas, and so forth; my own view is that individual areas can be characterized as having specific functions that will reliably be reflected by PET activation, but that's not the only possibility. With PET the situation is particularly tricky because most PET work involves subtracting blood flow in one condition from blood flow in another. Depending on the nature of the baseline task, different patterns of activation will be evident.

MG: If there are constraints in understanding lesion data and hemisphere data, I suppose there are constraints in interpreting PET data. You have recently jumped into the PET arena and have published a fascinating report that visual imagery involves primary visual cortex. Give a quick synopsis of that study and tell us what you think the data can mean.

SK: The PET research on imagery that we've conducted, in conjunction with Nat Alpert and the MGH group, has centered on resolving the "imagery debate." As I mentioned at the outset, this debate focused on the nature of the internal representations underlying the experience of imagery. Specifically, when one experiences a visual mental image, is a picture-like "depictive" representation being processed? My colleagues and I argued that—miraculously!—introspection can sometimes reveal properties of the functional representations. To investigate this issue, we showed that topographically mapped visual cortex is activated when one forms visual mental images, even if one's eyes are closed. In addition, we found that spatial properties of images systematically affect the activation in these areas: When subjects visualized letters so that they seemed to subtend large visual angles, the centroid of activation shifted toward the anterior portions of this topographically mapped area, relative to when the subjects visualized letters so that they seemed to subtend small visual angles. In fact, the coordinates of these centroids were reasonably close to where they should be, based on the estimated "size" of the imaged letters (using techniques I developed in the 1970s to estimate the "visual angle" subtended by imaged objects). I am now fairly confident that the activated area in medial occipital cortex probably is area 17, especially given results from later work with functional magnetic resonance imaging (fMRI, e.g., from Ogawa and Tank, from Le Bihan and Turner, and from a collaboration we have with Belliveau at the MGH); this technique allows more precise localization within a single individual.

What do such findings mean? It is well known that most areas in the visual system (of the macaque) that have afferent connections to other areas also receive efferent connections from them; the connections are reciprocal. I argue that visual information is stored in a type of compressed code, and that imagery occurs when visual memories cause activation to flow backward in the visual system, along the efferent connections, to reconstruct a pattern in topographically organized cortex. By so doing, the shape, color, and spatial properties of objects are made accessible for additional processing. For example, your visual memory of a German Shepherd dog is probably stored in inferior temporal cortex using some kind of population code, which specifies shape by a vector defined over a large set of neurons with complex response properties. If I ask you whether the dog's ears are pointed, or whether the ears sit on the top or sides of its head, or whether they protrude above the top of its head, you will probably generate a visual mental image to reconstruct the actual spatial layout. Once you've generated the image, you can "take a second look" and reinterpret information that was only implicit in your stored memories. As this view implies, we did in fact find activation in inferior temporal cortex and a variety of other areas that presumably are used in generating and interpreting visual images.

MG: So, are you bothered by the fact that there are findings suggesting mental imagery goes on in other cortical areas such as the frontal lobes?

SK: Not at all; this is exactly as we predicted. We have argued that imagery involves depictive representations, which occur in topographically mapped regions of the occipital lobe, but imagery also involves nondepictive long-term memory representations (which we think are stored in the inferior temporal lobe) and lots of processing (including in frontal areas) to generate and use images. As Marr argued, the brain apparently implements many, very specialized "computations," which may be carried out in different regions. Any complex activity, such as imagery, perception, or memory, is likely to be accomplished by a host of relatively simple computations that work in concert. Our PET results show that a *system* of areas is involved in carrying out imagery. So, for imagery, we find that areas in the frontal lobes that are used to direct attention to key aspects of visual stimuli are also activated when one generates images. We hypothesize that high-resolution images are generated by activating visual memories of individual parts or properties, and "placing" them in the appropriate relative locations. This process, we argue, relies on the same machinery used to shift attention to search for a distinctive part of an object during perception. Other imagery activities, such as mental rotation or image maintenance, would use other combinations of simple component processes. So, from this perspective we expect different tasks to result in different patterns of brain activation.

MG: Given the large number of assumptions, is this technology really useful for cognitive neuroscience?

SK: All methods rely on lots of assumptions, so that fact alone can't be a criticism of PET or fMRI per se. It's still too soon to know what the critical assumptions are for these techniques; I suspect that the best way to find out is to keep using the techniques and vary various parameters, discovering what is and is not important. Is the technology useful? Depending on the question one asks, different things count as answers. If one wants to know whether two tasks rely on the same processing, then showing that the same pattern of brain activation occurs during both can help one to answer that question. If one wants to know whether two processes are the same or different, then finding separate patterns of activation for them can answer the question. In my view, the new scanning technologies are likely to play an even greater role in cognitive neuroscience as we begin to characterize what distinct areas of the brain do (e.g., anterior cingulate cortex, area 46, etc.); once we have characterized what an area does, we then can start to draw inferences about how subjects perform a task that activates that area. Given that the area is activated, one has evidence that a specific process is used to perform the task. This sort of reasoning is not always going to be simple or straightforward, however, because a number of different processes may turn out to be supported by the same tissue, or the function of a given area may turn out to depend in part on what other areas are doing, but the more we understand about what an area of the brain does, the more we can learn about a task that activates that area. But again, let me stress, I think convergent evidence is the way to go; there is no Royal Road to understanding how the brain gives rise to the mind.

MG: PET, then, will play a greater role in sharpening ideas about cognitive models of imagery or memory or whatever. I guess you don't see it playing a role in actually instructing the neuroscience side of the equation, namely the physiological mechanism active in enabling a cognitive state. After all, when activation is detected, it is not at all clear whether it reflects inhibition or excitation at the synaptic level.

SK: I'm no expert on the physiology of PET, but I think it's too soon to foreclose any specific use of it. PET may well turn out to be a tool that can be used to determine whether a particular activation reflects net inhibition or excitation. I would argue that the problem of characterizing neural activity will be solved only by developing and testing specific theories. In cognitive neuroscience, we are trying to develop theories of what sets of neurons do. In my view, as we understand how specific components of the functional architecture are implemented in the brain, we will necessarily come to understand more about the neural substrate. Our ignorance of whether activation reflects net excitation versus inhibition pales beside our ignorance of what are the consequences of a local pattern of activation for processing in the system as a whole. The ambiguous nature of activation is actually much worse than you note: It's not simply that we don't know whether the activity reflects net inhibition or excitation at the synaptic level, it's that we don't know what the area is doing (is it activating stored information? releasing some other area from inhibition? selectively activating a process implemented elsewhere? transforming input into a different kind of output? etc.) and we don't know how the area is carrying out this computation. PET is one method that will help us to answer such questions, and in so doing we will understand more about the brain itself. PET will not be the only tool to advance our knowledge of neural activity, and probably couldn't do it alone, but it will be one source of convergent evidence.

MG: But for the cognitive modeler, the details of what is happening at a synaptic level are not important. Right?

SK: To the contrary, in my view the two enterprises—understanding cognitive processing and understanding the neural substrate—mutually inform each other; they are different facets of the same problem. It is clear that further insights about neurophysiology and neuroanatomy inform the cognitive end (for example, Rockland's recent findings of direct connections from area TE to area V1 have clear implications for theories of imagery), and as we come to understand the nature of cognitive processing, that should inform theories of the neural substrate (e.g., my view of what V1 does has been changed by our PET results). A more detailed understanding of the neural activity that underlies a specific pattern of activation will aid cognitive modeling. Indeed, someone wanting to build a "realistic" neural network model will very much want to know patterns of excitatory and inhibitory interactions at the synaptic level; and even questions about the nature and organization of processing subsystems will be easier to answer as we know more details about the neural events that produce specific activation and the specific anatomic connections among local portions of the brain.

MG: So, what's the next step if you've been working on visual mental imagery for over twenty years now; what do you see for the next twenty years?

SK: We've begun to make a dent in understanding the mechanisms that allow us to produce and use mental images, but it is clear that this is only a dent. My work has become increasingly focused on understanding the role of specific content in directing and modulating processing. For example, a major question that has received too little attention concerns the role of imagery in emotion. Why do vivid images often accompany highly emotional memories? What roles do these images play? How does the imagery system that we've begun to characterize interact with the neural systems that underlie emotion? My current goal is to use PET and fMRI to try to understand (at a relatively coarse level) the circuitry that causes one's palms to sweat when one visualizes a threatening scene (e.g., teetering on a narrow trail etched into the side of a very steep mountain). As part of this effort, I would like to understand the role of imagery in classical conditioning. Thirty years ago this would have seemed a very odd juxtaposition indeed, but it is now possible to study such questions—and perhaps even to begin to answer them!

MG: Thank you.

10

Qualia
Daniel C. Dennett

Daniel Dennett was educated at Harvard and Oxford, receiving his D. Phil. in 1965. After six years at University of California, Irvine, he moved to Tufts, where he is Distinguished Professor of Arts and Sciences and Director of the Center for Cognitive Studies. He is the author of articles on many issues in artificial intelligence, psychology, and cognitive ethology, as well as in philosophy. His books are Content and Consciousness *(1969),* Brainstorms *(1978),* The Mind's I *(with Douglas Hofstadter, 1981),* Elbow Room *(1984),* The Intentional Stance *(1987), and* Consciousness Explained *(1991). His latest book is* Darwin's Dangerous Idea *(1995).*

MG: You are known both as a philosopher and as a cognitive scientist. How do think of yourself? Where does the one role stop and the other start?

DD: I consider myself a philosopher. Before the twentieth century philosophers often became quite embroiled in the science of their day (with mixed results, of course!), so my involvement with the details of cognitive science is not such an anomaly as it may appear when it is contrasted with the more recent stereotype of the philosopher who just sits in his armchair and claims to figure it all out from first principles.

Philosophy of science is one of the strongest—I think the strongest—of the subdisciplines in philosophy these days, and there are philosophers of physics who are quite at home in the lab or the farthest reaches of theory, philosophers of biology whose contributions mingle fruitfully with those of the more theoretically minded evolutionists, and so forth. I am trying to do the same thing in cognitive science. My goals and projects differ in two ways from those of some other philosophers working this territory.

First, unlike some philosophers of cognitive science, I do not view my role as solely what we might call "meta-criticism"—analyzing and criticizing the theories, arguments, and concepts of the scientists. On the contrary, I aspire to create, defend, and confirm (or disconfirm) theories that are directly about the phenomena, not about theories about the phenomena. The philosophers' meta-criticisms are often important clarifiers and exposers of confusion, and as such are—or should be—unignorable contributions, but I myself would also like to make more direct contributions to theory.

Second, and following from this, I don't consider cognitive science to be simply a mine from which philosophers of mind can extract valuable support for their purely philosophical theories. It is that, of course, and the insights gleaned from cognitive science have transformed—if not quite killed—traditional philosophy of mind. But what philosophers of mind sometimes fail to appreciate is that the scientists are just as susceptible to conceptual confusions as the "layman" and hence the fruits of their research cannot be taken neat and used as a stick to beat sense into the benighted layman. There are at least as many closet Cartesians and uncritical believers in "qualia" among the scientists as among the uninitiated, for instance, and these scientists have something to learn from philosophy (whether they like it or not!).

I don't have a lab or do experiments, but I do devote a lot of effort to proposing experiments (or perhaps I should say "provoking" experiments) and to redesigning and criticizing experiments. And I have discovered, of course, that there is no substitute for direct experience in the lab. Many times I have thought I understood a series of experiments from reading the literature on them, only to uncover a fairly major misapprehension on my part when I actually witnessed the paradigm, or became an informal subject. Live and learn. That's why, although I am a philosopher, not an experimental scientist, I can't do my work well without poking my nose in the labs. Besides, it's much more interesting than just reading philosophy journals.

MG: So in a sense the philosopher's role is to prevent thought disorders among scientists. Likewise a simple empirical fact can raise havoc with a philosopher's theory of mind, requiring that the philosopher keep abreast of recent discoveries. Before going further, can we get out on the table what you mean by qualia?

DD: I thought you'd never ask. Qualia are the souls of experiences. Now, do you believe that each human experience has its own special and inviolable soul?

MG: What are you getting at? What on earth does that even mean?

DD: That's just my wake-up call for people who think they know what qualia are. It's frustrating to learn that in spite of my strenuous efforts, people keep using the term "qualia" as if it were innocent. Consider a parallel: According to Descartes (and many churches), the difference between us and animals is that animals have no souls. Now when Darwin showed that we are a species of hominid, did he show that there really aren't any people after all—just animals? If Darwin is saying we're just animals, he must be denying we have souls! So he must be saying that people aren't really people after all!

That's silly, but it isn't as if we didn't sometimes talk that way:

"You're behaving like an animal!"

"But I *am* an animal!"

or:

"They treated us as if we were animals."

In spite of tradition, the very real and important differences between people and (other) animals are not well-described in terms of the presence or absence of souls fastened to their brains. At least I would hope most of your readers would agree with me about that. Similarly, the differences between some mental processes and others are not well-described in terms of the presence or absence of qualia—for what are they? Not only is there is no agreed-upon definition among philosophers; controversies rage. Until they get settled, outsiders would be wise to avert their gaze, and use some other term or terms—some genuinely neutral terms—to talk about properties of subjective experience.

In fact the term "qualia"—which is, after all, a term of philosophical jargon, not anything established in either common parlance or science—has always had a variety of extremely dubious connotations among philosophers. Denying there are qualia is more like denying there are souls than like denying that people are much smarter than animals. If that makes "qualia" sound like a term one would be wise to avoid, good!

To put it bluntly, nobody outside of philosophy should take a stand on the reality of qualia under the assumption that they know what they're saying. You might as well express your conviction that trees are alive by saying they are infused with élan vital. So when Francis Crick, for instance, says that he believes in qualia, or when Gerald Edelman contrasts his view with mine because his view, unlike mine, allows for qualia, these pronouncements should be taken with more than a grain of salt. I'd be very surprised if either Crick or Edelman—to take two egregious examples—believes in what the philosophical fans of qualia believe in. If they do, they have a major task ahead of them: sorting out and justifying their claims against a mountain of objections they've never even considered. I would think they'd be wise to sidestep the mess.

I fear I'm losing the battle over the term "qualia," however. It seems to be becoming the standard term, a presumably theory-neutral way of referring to whatever tastes and smells and subjective colors and pains are. If that's how it goes, I'll have to go along with the gang, but that will just make it harder to sort out the issues, since it means that all the controversies will have to be aired every time anybody wants to ensure that others know what is being asserted or denied. Too bad. Don't say I didn't warn you.

MG: Well, OK. These things happen. "Qualia" is doomed to mean the feeling about the specialized perceptual and cognitive capacities we humans enjoy. Put directly, should we not distinguish between the task of characterizing the cognitive operations of the human mind and the (here we go) qualia we have about them?

DD: Certainly we should divide and conquer. So we should distinguish between the task of characterizing *some* of the cognitive operations of the human mind, and the rest (which we conveniently set aside till later); but if we call the latter "qualia" and think that they are somehow altogether different from the "cognitive operations" we are studying now, we prejudge a major question.

Take experienced color, every philosopher's favorite example of a quale. Suppose what interests you as a cognitive scientist are the differences in people's responses to particular colors (Munsell color chips will do for standard stimuli, at least for this imaginary example). But instead of looking at such familiar measures of difference as size of JNDs, or latency of naming, or choice of color words (where does each subject's "pure red" lie on the spectrum, etc.), or galvanic skin response, or some ERP difference, suppose you looked at variations in such hard-to-measure factors as differences in evoked memories, attitude, mood, cooperativity, boredom, appetite, willingness to engage in theological discussion ... you name it. Until you've *exhausted* all these imponderable effects, you haven't covered all the "cognitive" or "disposition-affecting" factors in subjective color experience, so there will be features of color experience, features of what it is like for each individual, that you are leaving out of your investigation. Obviously. But if you then call these unexamined residues "qualia" and declare (or just assume) that these leftovers are somehow beyond the reach of cognitive science, not just now but forever, you are committing a sort of fallacy of subtraction. There need be nothing remarkable about the leftovers beyond their being leftovers (so far). When some qualia freak steps up and says, "Well, you've got a nifty account of the cognitive side of color vision, but you still have a mystery: the ineffable what-it-is-likeness of color qualia," you needn't concur; you are entitled to demand specifics.

To cut to the chase, I once got Tom Nagel in discussion to admit that given what he meant by "qualia," there could be two identical twins whose scores on every test of color discrimination, color preference, color memory, effects of color on mood, etc., came out the same, and there would *still* be a wide-open question of whether the twins had the same color qualia when they confronted a particular Munsell chip! (By Nagel's lights, neither twin would have any grounds for supposing that now he knew that he and his twin brother had the same color qualia.) Nagel's position is an available metaphysical position, I guess, but I hope it is obvious that it doesn't derive any plausibility from anything we have discovered about the nature of color experience, and hence no cognitive neuroscientist needs to be shackled by any such doctrine of qualia.

By the way, this should make it clear why I said qualia were the souls of experiences. Nagel's position is parallel to that of the vitalists of yore who, after being shown all the details of metabolism, biochemistry, etc., still held out that Life was not being accounted for: "You still haven't explained the ineffable aliveness of these organisms!"

There are obviously large families of differences and similarities in experience that are best ignored at this stage of inquiry—no one can get a good scientific handle on them yet. One can admit that there is a lot more to color experience, or any other domain of subjectivity, than we have yet accounted for without thereby endorsing the dubious doctrine that qualia are properties that elude objective science forever. But that doctrine is the standard destination of all the qualia arguments among philosophers.

MG: So what is the task of the future students of the problem of consciousness? What should be the content of their research? Is it to solve the brain mechanisms enabling, say, problem solving, and along with that will come some deeper understanding of the old ineffable qualia?

DD: That's roughly right, in my opinion. Here is one place—not the only one, of course—where cognitive neuroscientists could take a hint from AI. The people in AI have almost never worried about consciousness as such, since it seemed obvious to them that if and when you ever got a system—an embodied robot, in the triumphal case—that actually could do all the things a person can do (it can reflect on its reflections about its recollections of its anticipations of its decisions, and so forth), the residual questions about consciousness would have fairly obvious answers. I have always thought they were right.

MG: The quip often heard about your book, *Consciousness Explained,* is that you explained it away. So, let me come at the problem from another angle. There can be little doubt most of our brain activity that enables us to do anything goes on outside the realm of our conscious experience. We hardly have access to the processes that allow us to be motoric, to create, to recall, and so on. We seem to know only about the products of these activities. What is that? What is it that is looking at all of these products?

DD: "We"? Who or what is this "we" you speak of who has or lacks access to various processes? A self is not a separate thing in the brain, with its own agenda and powers, which is made privy to some brain processes and not others. There is nothing that is, as you say, "looking at" all these products, though I agree that it is very hard to keep this strange fact in place as one thinks about what's going on. The various *effects* of conscious access (or lack thereof) have to be shown to be the natural and indeed constitutive outcome of the activities and processes themselves, traced out through all their interactions. A sure sign of residual Cartesianism in any model is when it describes processes leading up eventually to some central transduction or threshold-crossing (or phase lock or induced synchrony), which is then declared, for reasons good or bad, to ensure consciousness for the product in question. At any such moment we must go on and ask the embarrassing question: "And Then What Happens?" That is, what account does the model give of what is thereby enabled by this putative onset of "access"? Most models give no account at all. The task of the cognitive neuroscientist, however, is not just to explain how one's favorite phenomena get all the way up to consciousness; to complete the task one has to explain what happens all the way *through* consciousness to eventual behavior (and behavioral dispositions, of course). Only then will we be able to see why and how the theory is a theory of consciousness at all.

The quip that my book ought to be titled *Consciousness Explained Away* is telling. Different readers no doubt have different grounds for saying it, but in any event it would perfectly express the attitude of one who had missed the whole point of the book—rather like somebody who might quip that Darwin's theory of evolution by natural selection didn't so much explain the design in the biosphere as explain it away. My theory of consciousness certainly doesn't explain everything about consciousness that needs explaining, but at least it has the right overall shape: it undertakes to show how each feature that people have taken consciousness to exhibit is either the effect of some mechanism or mechanisms the operation of which can be understood without any tincture of consciousness, or else is the figment of an inflated or otherwise mistaken claim. I don't see how any other *sort* of theory of consciousness could presume to have explained it. Has liquidity been explained away by the physicists because, in their final account, they don't attribute liquidity to anything at the atomic level? The physicists have left out the wetness, and I've left out the qualia. On purpose.

MG: But in the case of physicists explaining away wetness, they can reconstruct every aspect of actual wetness from their molecular theory. They can show how surface tension necessarily creates drops, how the rolling and tumbling among molecules of a liquid state allow it to pour and assume the shape of a container, and so on. But in the case of consciousness, can your theory actually show mechanically why my pain "hurts" me (as opposed to merely changing my goals and behavior) and that apples actually "look red" to me (as opposed to merely contrasting with leaves and reminding me of firetrucks)?

DD: You are certainly right to stress that the effects still in need of explanation are many, but there is a fatal—and common—mistake to avoid here: arriving at the "conclusion" that after "all" the effects of this sort are explained, there will be some inexplicable residue. How do some people reach this imagined conclusion? By imagining themselves to engage in a process of something like subtraction: "Here am I, looking at the apple, and reflecting on how wonderfully red it appears. Now I subtract my reflections, my dispositions, my changes in mood, my memories, my . . . and I ask: 'what's left?' and I 'see' that there is still something left over: the very intrinsic redness of it all!" That is not an argument; you couldn't prove anything with such an exercise of the imagination, if only because there's really no way you can prevent the very items you take yourself to have subtracted away from somehow returning surreptitiously to fuel your sense that something is still there.

Compare it to the naive but strangely compelling attitude some people have toward dollars, encapsulated in the American tourist's query: "What does it cost in *real* money?" Such a person finds it easy to believe that marks and francs and pounds and yen have value only in virtue of their exchange rate with dollars, but they persist in thinking that dollars are different; dollars have *real* value, *intrinsic* value! These people find it very hard to believe that there isn't "something left over" when they've subtracted all the merely dispositional features of dollars— their instrumental value in exchange for goods, services, and other currencies. They are wrong, of course. I am claiming that the hardcore qualophiles are making the same sort of mistake.

MG: So this brings us to your own strategy of discovering new insights in the stuff of conscious experience. Are you not trying to build a cognitive/conscious agent at MIT? Tell us about that project and, in particular, speak to the point of Searle and others that building agency out of anything save biological material is a doomed enterprise.

DD: Cog, undoubtedly the most ambitious, most humanoid robot yet attempted, is being designed and built at the AI Lab at MIT, by a team of graduate students under the direction of Rodney Brooks and Lynn Andrea Stein. I am playing an advisory role on the team, and, in the process, learning all my heart desires about the immense technical difficulties of building actual robots.

Cog is to have an extended "infancy," not growing in size, but developing many of the competences that human infants develop, from thousands of hours of embodied "experience" in the real world. Cog is adult-size, with a movable torso, head, and arms, but lacking legs. Cog is bolted at the "hips" to a fixed pedestal, which solves the problem of providing huge amounts of electrical power and multifarious connections to Cog's massively parallel brain, which is telephone-booth-sized, without a cumbersome trailing umbilical cable. Cog's fingers, hands, and arms have approximately the same amount of "give" as their human counterparts, and Cog's eyes saccade at near-human rates (3, not 4 or 5, saccades a second, with comparable speed of saccading and dwell-time). Cog's eyes are composed of two tiny TV cameras, a high-resolution foveal camera mounted on top of a wide-angle parafoveal camera. Among the features of human vision that have to be modeled in Cog are the problems of integrating the VOR, head and skeletal motion in addition to eye movement, vergence control, motion detection, "pop-out" for various importance features, face-recognition, . . . the list keeps growing, of course. Achieving human-level hand-eye coordination is a central goal, but before that can be addressed, we have to ensure that Cog won't poke its eyes out with inadvertent motions of its arms! So a pain system, and innately "hard-wired" (actually software-controlled, of course) avoidance of such mischief is a high priority.

It is still too early to say just how far, and how fast, the Cog project will go, but at least the problems being addressed are real problems of real cognitive science, shockingly oversimplified from some perspectives—from the standard perspectives of functional neuroanatomy, for instance—but still orders of magnitude more realistic than other modeling efforts in AI. The Cog project is controversial among people working in AI, and some outspoken critics think it will come to much less than the fascinated public (and science journalists) expect, so much less that it is an unwise undertaking at this time. I disagree, but of course I am biased. For me, it is like being given Aladdin's lamp: with any luck, I will soon know whether some of my favorite inchoate ideas can be turned into working models. a task that is way beyond my own technical competence, but well within the range of the brilliant young people on this team.

One of my advisory roles is directing members of the team to crucial ideas, phenomena, and problems, from other areas of cognitive science that they have not yet encountered on their own. They are primarily engineering students, but quick studies with voracious curiosity, undaunted by any technicalities. I mention this in particular, because any cognitive neuroscientists who have a burning conviction that Cog will never work without X (where X is something they know all about) are invited to try to convince the Cog team (through me) that they are right. In other words, short, argument-packed letters that begin, "If I were designing Cog's vision system [motor-control system, audition, memory, pain system], I'd make sure that it exploited . . ." will be carefully read. We don't think we already know all the answers about how to do it.

One thing we're sure about, though, is that John Searle's idea that what you call "biological material" is a necessity for agency (or consciousness) is a nonstarter. Oh, it might turn out, for largely boring reasons, that electric motors are such poor substitutes for muscles (made of organic polymers, artificial or natural), that any truly effective humanoid robot must have organic muscles. And I suppose it might turn out for similarly boring reasons that silicon chips, no matter how massively parallel, simply cannot do all the transformations (= computations) that the organic materials in our nervous system do, but if this turns out to be so, it would not be any confirmation of Searle's vision, since he explicitly detaches the "causal powers of the brain" that he is interested in from all such issues of real-time control. He concedes (perhaps unwisely) that a silicon brain could control a humanoid body exactly as well and as fast as an organic brain. If that is so, Cog can get by just fine with silicon chips, which is what we are gambling on.

MG: But even if qualia or subjective experience can be explained right out of science, aren't they ineliminable from the very way we think about ourselves and each other, and especially from ethical thinking? The whole argument about animal rights has to do with whether the fish actually feels pain when it bites the hook, or just flops around reflexively. If I cut the cord to Cog, then I'd be guilty of vandalism if it didn't have any conscious experiences, but I'd be guilty of murder if it did. So it seems like the sense of consciousness you want to explain away really does make a difference!

DD: I agree that it is ethical considerations that make the question of pain, and hence consciousness, so important, and this is exactly why it is not just wrong but deeply immoral to mislocate the issue in doctrines that are systematically unconfirmable and undisconfirmable. If the question of whether the fish feels pain is declared to be unknowable in the limit of scientific inquiry then how on earth could the injunction not to cause unnecessary pain be so important? What is important can be observed, shared, noticed—if not yet, then by an extension of investigations we already know how to conduct. I think the idea that pain is, as it were, a morally important but nevertheless unmeasurable "quantity" is a pernicious oversimplification (as I argued in the section called "Minding and Mattering" at the end of *Consciousness Explained*). In the case of Cog, I agree entirely that the time may well come when our moral duties *to Cog* (and not merely to Cog's owners) become a very serious consideration, for exactly the same reasons they are a consideration for any experimenters working with animals (including human beings). There has already been considerable discussion about this among members of the Cog team and interested onlookers. And let me end on a reassuring note: the errors will almost certainly be on the side of oversolicitousness. People—even the sophisticated technocrats who make robots—are amazingly easily moved to sympathy, empathy, concern. A little "eye" contact is overwhelmingly moving. If Cog "works" at all, you can rest assured that Cog will have plenty of ardent guardians, eager to weigh Cog's own interests and needs in any decision making.

MG: So your position is there is really no conceivable argument against a functionalist view, given our knowledge and beliefs about the explanatory power of modern science?

DD: Oh, I'm sure we can *conceive* of arguments against functionalism; it's just that I haven't encountered any good ones yet. But who knows what argument will come along tomorrow? I certainly don't want to encourage neuroscientists to turn a deaf ear to philosophical arguments—open-minded skepticism seems to me to be the appropriate attitude.

MG: Well, laboratory scientists are always fascinated with philosophy and philosophers. One thing that always comes across is how trained and expert philosophers are in the art of argument and in the distinctions they insist on making. At the same time, sometimes it is felt philosophers and in particular the modern philosophers of mind stake out positions and then consider new data from their personal perspective, not with the aim of validating or invalidating their view but with seeing how to keep their view intact given the data. Now this is not an impudent charge. It is a reflection of the fact that since we are a light year or two away from truly understanding how the brain does its business, this is the only practical way to survive. Or would you reject this interpretation of current behavior?

DD: I see it a little differently. Scientists just as often as philosophers defend their positions until the last dog is hanged, and so they should. You don't abandon a promising theory in the face of a single unforeseen counter-instance if you can think of a way to refine or adjust your theory. Human nature being what it is, however, we are often tempted to preface such a regrouping with "What I meant all along was . . ." instead of, "What I should have said was . . ." But philosophers are actually in a slightly different position from other theorists. We philosophers have a delicate balancing act to perform: as would-be analyzers of concepts, among the truths we strive to uncover are conceptual truths, and these shouldn't be any more vulnerable to straightforward empirical disconfirmation (or confirmation) than their more obviously a priori brethren, mathematical truths. So it is entirely appropriate that we try to construct theories that leave most of the empirical options wide open—it is not our job to fill in all those details. So any time anything we say appears to be flatly at odds with some empirical discovery, something has to give. Most often, the right thing to do is to re-express the philosophical point in a way that shows that it was not foreclosing on the discovery after all. And almost as often, the nonphilosophical critics actually *have* misinterpreted the philosopher's position, so a certain amount of "you've misunderstood me" is perfectly legitimate! Suppose a bridge collapses, and we confront the geometer who advised us on its construction: "We thought you said triangles were rigid figures!" we complain. "And so they are," he replies, undaunted by the pile of twisted steel members. "These are *former* triangles." What else should the geometer say—that triangles are *unusually* rigid, or that they are rigid unless undue strain is put on them? Those aren't truths of geometry. Notice that truths of geometry do explain why bridges made of triangles are sturdier than bridges without them—and these explanations embody testable empirical predictions. The geometer isn't copping out, and philosophers *need not* be copping out when they point to an escape hatch in their definitions.

MG: Finally, then, help us distinguish the major views of current philosophers of mind. You, as the supreme functionalist, hold that an artifact that was complex enough could have all the properties of consciousness. The Searle school would reject this and maintain that there is something special about neural tissue that makes it a necessary substrate or source of consciousness. And finally, the Churchland school maintains that in order to explain how brain processes are conscious processes, you have to descend to principles at the molecular level. Is that roughly right? Are there other contenders we should know about? Where does that leave the cognitive neuroscientists? Are we waiting for you to add to the debate or are you waiting for us?

DD: It's interesting to see just how the philosophical disputes appear to you—and no doubt to your colleagues. Let me suggest a few revisions. In fact, I see myself in agreement with the Churchlands about everything except minor details, mainly of emphasis and method. Unlike them, I am simply agnostic about how deep into the particular details of neuroanatomy or neurochemistry we will have to go to get models that work—that can have the input-output functions required of minds. Even if we do have to go to the molecular level, I'll still consider functionalism unscathed; it will just have turned out that there are many *less* ways to skin the cat than I had supposed! I recently conjectured in a playful spirit that it *might* even turn out that just as some of the microscopic endoparasites in our gut play a well-nigh ineliminable role in our digestion, so other macromolecular parasites in our nervous systems might be required for cognition! Unlikely, surely, but as a worst-case scenario, it shows that functionalism is not *committed* to any particular "high level" of modeling. If Penrose and Hameroff are right—and

I'll eat my hat if they are—functionalism will have to descend to the quantum level to find its proper footing. It turns out that you can make quite serviceable artificial hearts without copying organic hearts at even the level of gross anatomy: artificial brains will no doubt have to be a lot more like organic brains to do their stuff, but how much is still an open question.

The Churchlands think they know what the right level for modeling minds in brains is. They might be right, but I'll reserve judgment. Given their views, they have expected more radical conceptual revisions to arise from neuroscience—overthrowing or "eliminating" the categories of folk psychology—while I have stressed that folk psychology (such everyday categories as belief, expectation, intention, dreaming, pain) are so powerfully predictive and useful that they are here to stay. So I have sought a more indirect accommodation of these categories within neuroscience. In the end it is not so much a factual or even theoretical disagreement between us as a tactical one, parallel to the simpler question of whether physicists should say that they have an explanation of "centrifugal force" or an explanation of why there really isn't any such force at all. (I think my disagreement with Pat Churchland over "filling in" is largely due to her misunderstanding my position, but that has been partly my fault—one of those cases where I have in fact prefaced my rejoinder with, "What I should have said was . . .") The main point of theoretical agreement between us is that what happens in the brain does *not* map neatly onto everyday notions of the mind (for instance, there is no Cartesian Theater in the brain, but it sure seems as if there is!), so materialism is a harder, more radical doctrine than some have thought.

Searle is not even in the same discussion. He claims that organic brains are required to "produce" consciousness—at one point he actually said brains "secrete" consciousness, as if it were some sort of magical goo—but since this is for him just an article of faith with no details, no models, no explanatory power, no predictions, it is hard to know what to say in response. Given the peculiar way he divorces his favored "causal powers" of brains from their control powers—the powers that permit them to accomplish discrimination and perception, underlie memory, guide behavior—his doctrine is conveniently untestable, now and forever. He and his followers do not shrink from this implication—they embrace it! To me, this is an unvarnished *reductio ad absurdum* of his position, and I marvel that anybody takes it seriously. Some people just love an insolvable mystery, I guess.

MG: Thank you.